Buddhism for Beginners

*A Practical Guide to Understand Buddhism,
Improve Mental Health and Find Peace in Your Life*

Gabriel Davidson

©Copyright 2021 – *Gabriel Davidson* - All rights reserved

The content contained within this book may not be reproduced, duplicated, or transmitted without direct written permission from the author or the publisher.

Under no circumstances will any blame or legal responsibility be held against the publisher, or author, for any damages, reparation, or monetary loss due to the information contained within this book, either directly or indirectly.

Legal Notice

This book is copyright protected. This book is only for personal use. You cannot amend, distribute, sell, use, quote or paraphrase any part, or the content within this book, without the consent of the author-publisher.

Disclaimer Notice

Please note the information contained within this document is for educational and entertainment purposes only. All effort has been executed to present accurate, up to date, and reliable, complete information. No warranties of any kind are declared or implied. Readers acknowledge that the author is not engaging in the rendering of legal, financial, medical, or professional advice.

Table of Contents

Introduction 4
Chapter 1. What is Buddhism, The First Buddha, and His Teachings 11
Chapter 2. The Life of the Buddha, The Three Values of Great Importance 16
Chapter 3. Symbols of Buddhism 22
Chapter 4. The Three Steps of the Way: 28
Chapter 5. The Five Aggregates 34
Chapter 6. Karma 42
Chapter 7: Rebirth, The Effects of Karma On the Next Life 48
Chapter 8. How to Practice Buddhism 54
Chapter 9. Guidelines for Practicing Buddhism 62
Chapter 10. The Roots of Evil 69
Chapter 11. Zen 77
Chapter 12. Buddhism and Christianity 85
Chapter 13. How to Find Enlightenment 92
Chapter 14. Combating Stress, Anxiety, and Depression with Buddhism 98
Chapter 15. Mudras to Combat Stress 105
Chapter 16. Start Your Day with Positive Motivations and Thoughts 113
Chapter 17. How Do I Begin to Practice Buddhism? 118
Chapter 18. What Are The 5 Precepts Of Buddhism? 122
Chapter 19. Why is Buddhism so Popular? 128
Conclusion 131

Introduction

Like other religions, Buddhism strives to help you find the answers to the more in-depth questions in life, like who am I? How can I be happy? But the wonderful thing about Buddhism is that it doesn't just ask you to do this and that, take the Buddha's word for it, and leave you to make sense of it all. Instead, Buddhism invites you to experience the nature of reality for yourself.

Once you are awakened or enlightened, you will experience your own internal and external reality. Inner reality is the part of you that remains constant and untouched by the outer world. Think of it as your anchor, which keeps you steady despite the chaos of the world around you. Think of it like the lotus, which remains untainted even as you float atop a polluted pond.

Buddhism's ultimate goal is to enable you to experience the awakening in the same way as the Buddha. If Buddhists don't worship a Supreme being, who was Buddha, then? To get straight to the point, Buddha was a man who lived in the 5th century BCE. He was immortalized in his disciples' memory because of the extraordinary life he lived.

He was part of the Shakya royal family clan in what is known today as Nepal. Although he was able to experience all the sensual delights the world had to offer, Prince Siddhartha, as he was then called, had deep compassion for his suffering brethren. Even when surrounded by luxuries, he understood the universality of sorrow. At age 29, he abandoned his wealth and all worldly pleasures. At the prime of his life, he chose to lead an austere existence. He wore a simple yellow garment and roamed the world in the quest for Peace, Truth, and Freedom from Suffering without a penny to his name.

For six years straight, he prayed and performed self-mortification. He tormented his body in an attempt to nourish the soul. He did this until he reached the point of emaciation. He ascertained that self-mortification only weakens the body and, consequently, exhausts the spirit. He then used this experience to form an independent path, the Majjhima Patipada, also known as the Middle Path.

Buddhist philosophy sharply diverged from another new religion that arose through similar circumstances: Jainism. It is also an ancient Indian religion that persists today and is often compared to Buddhism due to the many overlaps in the teachings they preach. Unlike Buddhism, however, Jainism espouses the virtues of asceticism through fasting and various other forms of penance. Jains also retains the belief in the soul, which they believe is found in every living creature on Earth.

That difference of viewpoint on asceticism is usually one of the most relevant factors for newcomers to these religions. Jainism can be significantly more challenging for some individuals to get into because of it. Buddhism is usually much more accessible and more comfortable to introduce into regular, contemporary life, giving it a significant advantage in the western hemisphere.

And much like Buddhism, Jainism sought to reform the faith and introduce a new philosophy to followers. These religions also mention a few similar principles and ideas, such as Reincarnation,

Karma, and other vital beliefs. However, despite the common origins and ground, Buddhism received much more official support than Jainism, which was probably the primary factor that allowed Buddhist teachings to spread further. It's also interesting that, just like the Buddha, Mahavir, one of the key figures in Jainism's creation, was also of noble birth.

Enlightenment came to him as he was meditating under the Bodhi tree. At this moment, he awakened to Buddhahood. From then on, he became known as Shakyamuni Buddha or "the awakened wise man of the Shakya clan." He did this all on his own, as a man with no supernatural powers.

For the next 45 years of his existence, the Buddha dedicated his life to preaching all over the North Indian subcontinent. He taught whoever was interested in living a life free from suffering. He was 80 years old when he died. The Buddha was mortal, yet he was godlike in every respect. However, although he had plenty of followers who revered him, he was never so arrogant as to refer to himself as a divine being.

The bottom line is that the Buddha was human, much like you and me. And like him, we, too, can achieve awakening. Like him, we again can become Buddhas. As a Bodhisatta (an aspiring Buddha), you also can follow that path the Buddha has led and, in so doing, find Truth, Peace, and Freedom from Suffering. The Buddha pointed out that we shall find salvation only by relying on ourselves, our capabilities, and our efforts. Simply put, you are your own savior.

A significant portion of the Buddha's journey, tribulations, and spiritual growth was a story of trial and error. It was a man who exercised his thoughts frequently while trying to fine-tune his philosophy before teaching others. His arrival at the Middle Way was the right course due to trial and error and Siddhartha's ability to be self-critical and think for himself. As you can see, the Buddhist affinity for critical thinking and the encouragement of skepticism is a direct reflection of how the Buddha himself traversed our troubled world and, as such, he led by example.

Buddhism is practical to the point of making numerous scholars and theologians not even recognize it as an organized, mainstream religion. There are different schools and traditions such that it is sometimes challenging to lump them into this one all-encompassing religion. Apart from the official sects and denominations, the openness to interpretation and personalized adoption by new adherents adds even more to Buddhism's versatility and diversity. Above all, Buddhism puts excellent faith in the individual and supports their natural inclination to think and question matters independently. It could be argued that some other religions go the opposite, dogmatic route, when they strive to hardcode their beliefs into the followers and do most of their thinking for them.

Buddhism recognizes that human beings possess the capacity to distinguish between good and evil. Simply put, Buddhism promotes the use of human intelligence as well as freedom to choose. You are encouraged to possess an open mind and an open heart. However, you are also encouraged to employ skepticism necessary. The Dalai Lama of Tibet couldn't have said it better: if the teachings suit you, then incorporate them into your life using the best of your capabilities. If, however, the instructions don't work for you, leave them be.

Buddha told his followers not to embrace everything he says because he said it. He advised them to test his teachings as though examining the authenticity of gold. If, after a thorough examination, his teachings proved to be accurate, then the followers may put them to practice.

This lack of aggressive indoctrination is why many argue that Buddhism is a scientific religion, if you will. The Three Marks of Existence, which form the core of the Buddhist way of perceiving the world are subject to scientific method and analysis. One can look into the concepts of impermanence, no-self, and even suffering and observe that they are indeed based in reality and very difficult to disprove. Unlike the assertions made by some of the other major religions, these claims are not hard to disprove because they are an unfalsifiable hypothesis. Instead, their sturdiness and plausibility stem from the fact that they result from a thorough analysis of the real world.

It has long been a powerful talking point of critics of religion that significant, monotheistic faiths make use of unfalsifiable hypotheses to solidify their claims for God's existence. It means making a proposition that cannot be disproven through logic or any scientific method by giving your request supernatural attributes that prevent it from being observed in nature. It is evident in Abrahamic religions, where God is described as impossible to hear, see, or feel, making it impossible to debunk His existence. Buddhism doesn't make use of this concept. Everything Buddhist teachings assert about our reality's circumstances is based on that reality, and anything that goes beyond it can and should be taken with a grain of salt. There is no punishment in Buddhism for not believing in other realms and similar propositions to the letter.

You can now see the appeal of Buddhism as a religion. It doesn't command. It doesn't demand. Buddhism doesn't provide you with the illusion that you were born free and then enslave you with set rules set in stone. More importantly, it does not mean you are loved and frightens you with eternal damnation ideas.

Instead, Buddhism encourages you to become the best version of yourself, utilize your inborn capacities as a human being, and maximizing these potentials to create a better world than the one you have found.

It's also essential that Buddhism doesn't seek to deliver you from the suffering of this life, utilizing fear and by barring you from temptation and possible sources of corruption through strict rules and notions of sin. Buddhist teachings don't teach their layperson followers that acquiring luxuries, pleasure, or enjoying life in other ways is an inherently terrible thing. Instead, Buddhists are taught not to attach themselves to transient possessions and sensory pleasures so their happiness and fulfillment don't depend solely on these things.

A Buddhist can thus acquire material gains, but he will know better than to equate these gains with existential fulfillment. Therefore, if these things are lost, this will create no-void or a deep sense of loss. No matter what we do and have in life, we should look within ourselves if we value spiritual growth and true satisfaction – this is the core message of wisdom.

Christianity is also one of three religions (the other two are Judaism and Islam) within the "Abrahamic tradition," They trace elements of their beliefs to Abraham, the father of Isaac and chosen by God as the father of nations. Abraham's story is among the most moving episodes of the Old Testament and has provided grist for innumerable scholars and exegetes over the centuries. But the specific Christian tradition begins with the coming of Jesus of Nazareth.

The Man and the Christ

We know about Jesus from the four gospels written by Mark, Matthew, Luke, and John (mostly from the first three, known as the Synoptic Gospels). According to tradition, he was born in humble circumstances: the son of a carpenter, born in a stable as his parents Joseph and Mary journeyed to Bethlehem to participate in the Roman census.

Chapter 1:
What is Buddhism, the First Buddha, and His Teachings

The name Buddhism derives from the title given by its followers, Siddharta Gautama. They called him the Buddha, meaning "the awakened" or "the enlightened one." Siddhartha Gautama lived around 500 BC. in northern India. The exact date of birth is unknown. He is commonly known in the Buddhist world as Shakyamuni, "the sage of the Shakya." These are the only historical facts we have about the Buddha. To learn about his teachings and his life, we must now look at him with Buddhist eyes.

His father had overprotected him: he saw no pain or suffering during his life in the castle. However, at this time in this life, he experienced the misery of the human condition for the first time. He saw a sick person, an older man, and a corpse. He asked his servant about it, and he said we are all destined to suffer that.

We must understand what questions Buddhism is trying to answer. The Buddha found the origin and solution of suffering. Then he told that this suffering arises because we are attached to things. This attachment comes from our ignorance and deception.

Then he talked about the solution to suffering. He said that Nirvana is the solution. Nirvana means to blow out. It merely is the extinction of all our desires that causes our lives to continue in a painful cycle. It's hard to think of Nirvana as a favorable destination from a Western perspective, but it's very desirable for Buddhists.

So, the Buddha tried to end human suffering. He answered no questions about the ultimate source of reality or our connection with the gods but only decided to solve a real problem he had. If you look at Buddhism from this perspective, it is difficult to talk about it as a religion. It is more of a philosophy and even shares aspects with modern psychology.

Mahayana Buddhists have fundamentally changed the beliefs and practices of traditional Buddhism. Some varieties of Mahayana worship heavenly Bodhisattvas and Buddhas. These are beings who have attained Enlightenment or are advanced practitioners of the path. They can intervene in this world and save people as if they were gods.

So, Buddhism is a very complicated tradition. It could be considered a religion or something else, depending on how we look at it.

Who is the Founder of Buddhism?

The basic practices of Buddhism are focused on meditation, but the methods of Zen Buddhism go even further. "Zen" originates from the Sanskrit word for contemplation. Everything can change into "zazen," which is the name of a Zen Buddhist contemplation method. Regular everyday practice is critical.

Buddhists from Monaco invest a great deal of energy pondering, and the part of Rinzai-Zen mostly utilizes the reflection on the koan. All professionals of Zen Buddhism look for illumination. Even though the thought is a fundamental piece of the activity, including different systems, it can help accomplish that objective.

Buddhism is religion dependent on the lessons of the Buddha known as the Dharma. The individuals who practice Buddhism are looking for a condition of complete edification known as nirvana.

This religion concentrated on Buddha's lessons by helping the sangha (meditator) in reflection to prepare the brain, dispense with affliction, and achieve nirvana. Mahayana Buddhism is practiced mainly in China, Korea, and Japan and includes mysticism and cosmology elements. Mahayana Buddhism is divided into two variants. Zen Buddhism, which focuses more on internalizing the spiritual journey and self-esteem, and the Pure Land, which teaches devotion to the Buddha Amitabha, are needed to reach nirvana.

Although Mahayana Buddhism heavily influences Tibetan Buddhism or Vajrayana, it forms another major discipline of the Buddhist faith. Tantric Buddhism, Vajrayana contains both text and writing, including Theraveda Mahayana Buddhism and Buddhist Tantra.

The Story of Siddhartha Gautama

Siddhartha Gautama was born below the Himalayan foothills in approximately 567 B.C.E. into the clan of Shakya, of which his father was chief. The story says that when Siddhartha Gautama was about 12 years old, the brahmins – members of the highest Hindu class, who were priests, teachers, and overall protectors of sacred learning – gave the prophecy that Siddhartha Gautama would either be a collective ruler or a celebrated holy man. His father kept him confined with the palace walls, where Siddhartha Gautama grew up in luxury. He was held within the castle walls to prevent him from becoming a holy man, also known as an ascetic. An ascetic one who practices self-denial to the extreme, leading a simple life while pursuing spiritual goals. It was not the life his father wanted for him, so he shielded his son from the outside world in hopes that Siddhartha Gautama would grow to be a great ruler.

Siddhartha Gautama was trained to swim and wrestle and train in archery and as a swordsman. Siddhartha Gautama eventually married his cousin, and they soon had a child, a son. It was not uncommon for royal families to marry among themselves because no other people were considered equal; they wanted to keep the royal line pure. Siddhartha Gautama's life was full and rich – in today's world, he would be one of those who have everything – wealth, luxury, a wife, and a child. With all of this happiness and luxury, what possible reason was there for Siddhartha Gautama to feel unsatisfied?

There was a longing inside of Siddhartha Gautama, a need to know more, a feeling of dissatisfaction with the life surrounding him. This longing led him to explore the world outside of the palace walls. In Kapilavastu, he came across three things: an older adult, a sick man, and a dead body being taken to the grounds for burning. Siddhartha Gautama had never seen such things before during his sheltered existence – he was not prepared; he did not understand what was happening before him. His chariot driver simplified it for him – every living being gets older, faces sickness, and eventually dies. This information caused great worry and uneasiness inside of Siddhartha Gautama.

He saw an ascetic dressed in a robe and carrying a bowl of a sadhu or a holy man on the way back to the palace. It was then that Siddhartha Gautama vowed to leave his life of luxury in the castle, as well as his wife and child, to find the solution to all of the suffering in the world. He never woke his wife and son up to bid them goodbye; instead, he said his goodbyes under cover of darkness, and he disappeared into the woods. Siddhartha Gautama used his sword to cut his long hair and donned a simple robe – an ascetic robe.

When Siddhartha Gautama decided to leave behind his royal life for that of an ascetic, he joined an entire group of men who had also left their lives behind. All of these men, including Siddhartha Gautama, were searching for blissful deliverance from individuality and suffering from the cycle of life – birth to death. Arada Kalama was his first teacher. Arada Kalama had more than 300 disciples learning his philosophy. He taught Siddhartha Gautama to train his mind to enter a state of emptiness, of nothingness. It took great discipline to reach this level of mindful peace. However, Siddhartha Gautama knew that this was not the liberation, the deliverance that he sought, so he left Arada Kalama's teachings, and he moved on to Udraka Ramaputra. Here, he was taught to enter a realm of his mind through concentration, a not conscious or unconscious kingdom. But again, he was dissatisfied with what he learned because he knew it was not true liberation.

Chapter 2:
The Life of the Buddha, The Three Values of Great Importance

They no longer have to sit through what Buddhists believe to be an endless cycle of suffering known as life. The path of Enlightenment has a few principles that are the foundation of Buddha's teachings. These principles are divided into three categories, which are prajna, sila, and samadhi.

Prajna

One of the first principles of the Buddhist path is prajna, also known as wisdom. Prajna is regarded as Enlightenment, which is the main focus of Buddhism. When it comes to prajna, understanding is a lot different than knowledge. Knowledge is what you know, a collection of facts. Wisdom comes out when you are most calm and pure. It's obtained through meditation and cultivation and comes at the end of your path.

Sila

The word sila translates to moral values and is essential in the path's progress as it's the foundation of qualities. There are two principles that sila is based on, and these are the principles of reciprocity and equality. When Buddhists talk about the direction of equality, they are speaking about the equality of all living things, including the equality of security and happiness.

Samadhi

Samadhi translates to mediation. As a Buddhist, you want to obtain pure freedom, which you can do through mental development. You need to purify the mind, and the only way to do this is through meditation or samadhi.

When you hear the word suffering, you may have images of pain and anger come into your mind, but they believe that all life is suffering in Buddhism. As humans, we feel the pain of loss, the emotions of sadness, happiness, disappointment, and so on. These emotions are manifestations of our mind, and they do not come from our inner selves. Because they do not come from our true selves, they are thought of as suffering. These are false feelings created by the meat of our brains, programmed into us by what our societal view has taught us. The way forward was through following the Noble Eightfold Path, which allowed people to be closer to Enlightenment's potential.

Currently, Buddhism is increasingly becoming a popular way of life for millions of people worldwide. Even those in the Western countries seek to follow The Middle Path because they find that it speaks to their heart. There is also the fact that traditional medicines do very little for the status quo. For example, if you are depressed or unable to deal with your feelings, scientists have established that the Buddhist way offers you a better and more permanent solution to your problems. Medical findings that explored the relationship between the Buddhist practice and how the brain operated found that Buddhist monks simultaneously use the brain's creative side and the brain's calculating side. They were, therefore, more open to creativity.

In a world where everything is always in motion, continually forcing us to move forward faster and more rapidly, many people feel the loss of a connection with nature. Although nature is all around us, even in the major cities, we have done to change Earth's pure form creates a disconnect from our minds. In Buddhism, you are connected to every natural thing in this world, and by practicing its teachings, you are brought back to that connection. It is an enormous draw for millions of people around the globe. You can think of it as connecting back to your roots.

If you are unsure of what this means, you only have to see what happens when you go somewhere inspiring. The feelings you experience don't just come from external stimuli. They come from your inner self-recognizing the joy that lies in that ever-moving thing called nature.

This lack of an invisible deity often speaks to those that cannot find solace or belief in other religions where God is the governing body. Though there are many tales and teachings in Buddhism, there is no one holy book such as the Bible or Quran. Instead, the "bible" of Buddhism can be found in every natural effect on the planet, from the leaves on the trees to the worms in the ground. They are the past story, but you don't need to look to the past to find Enlightenment.

Moreover, the belief system of Buddhism can be described as "large-minded." It is not uncommon to find those of different religious backgrounds meditating together at various Buddhist centers, especially in the western world. Enlightenment, in Buddhism, is not based on who you believe created you, but rather by opening your mind enough to allow yourself to shine through. Once it is reached, all the answers you seek on creation will be known to you. Therefore, your title of faith is of no concern, though those who strive for Enlightenment usually find themselves identifying as Buddhist or other similar namesakes. Instead, they only explain if asked.

Dharma

Dharma is the doctrine and cornerstone of the philosophy of these religions. In the practical sense, it encompasses ethics, rituals, obligations, code of conduct, and virtually anything else that comes into a devout follower's life. The Sanskrit word "dharma" has proven difficult to translate directly, but its meaning is relatively concise in Buddhism. Dharma denotes "cosmic law and order," one of the most common translations of the word. The same term is also ascribed to all that the Buddha has taught to his followers – the Buddhist dharma. Therefore, it's not uncommon for "dharma" and "the Buddha's teaching" to be used interchangeably.

Interestingly, various Hindu scriptures and teachings have spoken of the Buddha and acknowledged his existence and life's work. Depending on the different Hindu traditions, the Buddha was more than just mentioned in passing. While followers of some traditions believe the Buddha to have simply been a holy man, others view him as one of Lord Vishnu's earthly incarnations, which would make him divine. However, as we proceed, you will find that this is the diametric opposite of how Buddhists perceive the Buddha because they tie no divinity concept to the Buddha.

The most significant overlap between Hindu's and Buddhists' beliefs is perhaps the concepts of Karma and rebirth. These are just some of the significant similarities, though, and the two major religions overlap even further in many other beliefs important to their philosophy. Meditation, for instance, is a crucial practice that Buddhists put great emphasis on, and the same holds for Hinduism. It illustrates that both religions' focus is primarily on the believer's inner state relates to the outside world. In that regard, both Hinduism and Buddhism also promote the virtue of detachment from all earthly things in a material as well as a mental sense.

Unlike Hinduism, however, Buddhism does not delve too deeply into the ceremonial or ritual practices found in most major religions. It might seem counterintuitive at first if you ascribe ritualistic connotations to meditation. That would be a very wrong way of looking at it because meditation has virtually nothing to do with rituals. A devout Buddhist works on his introspection and strives to perfect it from one day to the next, and you will see why as you read more.

The spread of Buddhist teachings was only gradual at first. But a great wind that would push the religion to new heights came when Buddhists received open support from Ashoka, the emperor. He held reign over the largest part of the Indian subcontinent in the 3rd century BCE as sovereign of the Maurya Empire. Ashoka was a great admirer of the Buddhist approach to spirituality, and he supported the faith with great enthusiasm. It is evident by inscriptions and carvings left behind him, which told of his support and Buddhism's subsequent spread. This support continued through those who descended from Ashoka, and the extensive empire ultimately managed to successfully spread the Buddhist truth far and wide, beyond its borders to the north. These efforts also facilitated Buddhism's spread into Sri Lanka, where the Theravada tradition maintains a firm foothold today. Buddhism was also spreading westward over the subsequent centuries, and it may have gone much further had its spread not been halted in Persia in the 3rd century CE.

Looking at things from a certain angle, it could also be said that Buddhism came about as a product of its zeitgeist. It was a time when more and more intellectuals of varying prominence levels began questioning the traditional Vedic teachings and philosophies throughout Ancient India, giving way too many new ideas, one of which was undoubtedly the philosophy of Siddhartha Gautama.

Chapter 3:
Symbols of Buddhism

Six symbols were used to represent Buddha in the early years of Buddhism. There was never an image of Buddha himself used until the Buddha statue, which wasn't created until after Buddha's death. Buddha's vision was never used in early art as it was said that he did not like to be revered as a person and was reluctant to accept images of himself. The six symbols used most often in early art were the Eight Spoked Wheel, the Bodhi Tree, an Empty Throne, Buddha's Footprints, The Lion, Deer, and Stupas.

The Eight-Spoked Wheel

The Buddha is known as the Wheel-Turner. It was he who set a new cycle of teachings into motion and changed the course of destiny. The eight spokes in the Eight-Spoked Wheel symbolize the Eightfold Noble Path. There are often three swirling segments illustrated in the hub of the wheel that represent the Triple Gem.

The wheel is often looked at in three parts, the hub, the spokes, and the rim. Many people consider each piece to relate to the Buddha practice aspect, with the seat representing discipline, the spokes representing wisdom, and the rim representing concentration.

The Bodhi Tree

It is the tree that Prince Siddhartha sat beneath when he reached enlightenment and became the Buddha. Tree worship had been a part of India's culture before Buddha came into existence, so the Bodhi tree's development to become a holy symbol was natural and isn't surprising.

An Empty Throne

The symbol of the throne is a reference to two distinct parts of who the Buddha was. First, it is a reference to Prince Siddhartha's royal ancestry. It is also a reference to the idea of Enlightenment being a spiritual kingship.

Buddha's Footprints

Traditionally, the footprints symbolize the physical presence of the Enlightened One. It is said that before his death, the Buddha left an imprint of his foot on a stone as a reminder of his presence on earth.

The Lion

Since the Buddha was a prince, it became a fitting symbol. Buddha's teachings are occasionally referred to as Lion's Roar to indicate his teachings' power and strength.

Deer

This symbol also has two origins. Buddha's first teaching was in the Deer Park, Sarnath. It was also said that Buddha's appearances were so wondrous and his presence so peaceful that even the animals came to listen to what he had to say.

Stupas

Stupas are a symbolic grave monument used to represent the enlightened mind of the Buddha. They have been being constructed since the early days of Buddhism. A stupa is a square base, a round dome, and a cone shape with a canopy. These monuments have been made in all shapes and sizes.

The Buddha Statue

The most commonly recognized Buddha symbol today is the Buddha statue. The first Buddha statue was created during 500-550 B.E. Before this time, there was no image of Buddha used as a symbol. Buddhists use the figure because they find that the image gives them a transparent role model on their paths towards their Enlightenment.

Buddha statues can be found in a variety of poses. He was sitting, standing, smiling, or laughing. His hands are also found in a variety of gestures, called mudras. Each of these postures and gestures carries a different symbolism and relates to varying qualities of the Buddha. These qualities include balance, compassion, grace, and wisdom, courage, and determination. A couple of examples of common mudras that are found on Buddhist statues are:

-The Gesture of Meditation: Both hands are resting on the lap with palms facing upwards;

-The Gesture of Fearlessness: The right hand is slightly elevated with the palm turned outwards; And

-The Gesture of Debate: Explaining the Buddha's teachings, with the hands raised and tips of the thumbs and forefingers touching each other.

Non-Buddhists often use the Buddhist statue in their home or business to encourage an atmosphere of well-being and calm. It is especially true of psychotherapists and alternative healers.

Offerings

While some people believe that Buddhists worship the Buddha statues, this is not the case. Buddhists bow and make offerings in reverence to the Buddha himself, not to the image. They are reflecting on the virtues of the Buddha and inspire to become like him. The Buddha images are not necessary for this reverence. They are used by many Buddhists who find them helpful in keeping their focus. There are five traditional offerings used to show respect to the Buddha, flowers, light from lamps or candles, incense, water, and food. Each of these offerings represents something different.

Flowers: Flowers are offered to the Buddha to signify the practice of generosity. They are also used as a reminder of how quickly things change and that nothing lasts forever.

Light from Lamps or Candles: Light is offered to signify wisdom. The beauty of the light is said to dispel ignorance. By providing light to the Buddha, one is reminded to lead their mind to wisdom and question all things around them.

Incense: Buddhists offer incense to the Buddha to signify moral ethics and discipline. It is meant to remind one to be peaceful towards all things.

Water: Water is used to signify purity. Since water is used to cleanse, by providing water to wash the Buddha, one also cleans their minds.

Food

Food is used to remind us to give our best to the Buddha. Since food has many tastes, it is used to signify "Samadhi," which is ambrosia to feed the mind.

Other Reformers

By this time, the dispute had spread across Europe, where it had social and theological impacts. In Germany, peasants wanted to participate in newfound religious freedom, and they also demanded social, political, and economic reform. They formulated twelve demands:

1. Each parish should choose its pastor.

2. Some forms of tithing (that is, church taxes) should be abolished.

3. Serfdom, the tying of peasants to the land, should be done away with.

4. Peasants should have the right to hunt and fish freely.

5. Peasants should be able to collect building materials and firewood voluntarily from forests.

6. Lords should stop imposing oppressive workloads.

7. Peasants should only work according to what is "just and proper" according to an agreement between lord and peasant.

8. Rents should be affordable.

9. There should be equal justice for lord and peasant.

10. Unfair division of land should be done away with.

11. The death tax should be abolished.

12. If any of these demands did not adhere to the word of God, they would be scrapped.

Chapter 4:
The Three Steps of the Way

A person who wants to enter Buddhism must first learn Buddhist morality and live accordingly. It is the first step, which is to cultivate character in one's behavior. Second, she should develop her mind with a wholesome attitude of thought. This step involves studying Buddhist scriptures and growing right views, free from ignorance and wrong ideas about life. The third step is to cultivate wisdom, or seeing through the illusions of existence.

By following these steps, a person will gradually develop the ability to see things as they indeed are. Even if she learns many Buddhist doctrines and understands them, if at the same time she does not cultivate morality and mental development of wisdom, the result will be like that of a blind person who can explain in detail what an elephant looks like but cannot distinguish between one side and another.

Morality

A mind clouded by ignorance cannot know reality; it imagines everything as permanent, pleasant, and satisfying. Ignorance breeds desire, anger, fear, and greed. There are only suffering existences; all worldly existence is impermanent. Pleasures are not at all permanent; they always change into something else. The ultimate goal of life is happiness, but even the happiest moments will change into suffering because all things are impermanent. It is why we suffer.

Buddhism teaches us to transform this unsatisfactory and painful world into a pure land by practicing morality, cultivating wisdom, and developing our minds to obtain peace of mind so that our body and speech can express nobility.

Without this transformation, society cannot avoid the suffering it experiences daily. Therefore, morality is the first step on the path to free ourselves from wholesome or unwholesome actions; this is called self-control. Through character, we can overcome our mental and spiritual weaknesses and realize the potential for the healthy development of mind, speech, and body. Once morality is developed, wisdom can be cultivated.

Wisdom

In Buddhism, wisdom is called prajna. It means understanding the true nature of reality through meditation. Some people say that Buddhism meditation does not exist; however, if someone goes to a Buddhist learning center for ten years without knowing about meditation or having any personal experience with it, that person will have learned nothing. Meditation is practiced to experience reality's true nature; this cannot be achieved without developing concentration and insight through a qualified teacher's technique.

When a person who desires to practice meditation learns the method from a qualified teacher, she begins by learning to sit properly. It helps to develop the power of concentration needed for the development of wisdom. It is why a practitioner must learn how to sit properly with her back straight and her head erect. She should also practice breathing exercises to help develop concentration, focusing on one subject uninterrupted for a long time.

This kind of concentration develops in two different ways:

1. through physical means (as in breathing exercises) and
2. through mental means (as in mantra recitation)

The result of physical concentration is peace and stability. The effect of mental concentration is wisdom, which depends on one's ability to focus the mind on a single subject for long periods without being distracted.

From the beginning, one should practice focusing on a small detail, such as a pebble or leaf or flower. After some time has passed, she can gradually expand her concentration to include more objects, such as branches of trees and then whole trees and so forth. The practitioner must continue to concentrate until the illusion created by her mind vanishes, and actual reality is revealed. It is called "no self," meaning that she will see everything as empty because she will realize that there is no entity within phenomena. In this way, she will see the true nature of reality.

In the beginning, we should learn about the proper method from someone who has mastered it and then practices until we can do it without thinking about how we are doing it.

Mental Development

The concentration method should include stopping all thoughts by focusing on one object until there are no longer any obstacles for attaining higher concentration levels. If you reach the proper concentration stage, when you hear a sound or see a form, you will not be distracted by it. If you are distracted, it is because your concentration is weak. If you are not distracted even by loud sounds, it means that you have attained the first level of attention called "access concentration."

After attaining access concentration, no matter what thoughts or feelings arise from your mind, continue to focus on your object. It is called the second level of engagement, "absorption concentration." No matter what kind of thought arises during absorption concentration, continue to focus on your object without being disturbed. It is called the third level of attention, "momentary concentration."

This practice is the only way to reveal impermanence, suffering, and non-self. If you do not practice meditation, you will never understand the true nature of reality. All Buddhas and Bodhisattvas, those who possess perfect Enlightenment, attained it through meditation. Without it, they could not have achieved Enlightenment.

The Buddha said that when someone attains mindfulness or clear comprehension through meditation, she can see things as they are without any obstacles in her mind. People must develop concentration to understand impermanence as the Buddha taught us to do in his first sermon about impermanence: "All phenomena are impermanent; work happily for your liberation. All phenomena are painful; work happily for your liberation."

To work happily for happiness, we should first work to be liberated from mental and physical suffering by practicing meditation. We also need to understand that all things are impermanent and empty; therefore, they cannot bring us real or lasting happiness. It is why the Buddha said, "All phenomena are impermanent; work happily for your liberation." Working to be liberated from the sufferings of birth, old age, sickness, and death is the only way to achieve true happiness.

Every spiritual teaching begins with concentration because developing concentration is what leads us to insight or understanding. Therefore, without engagement, there can be no insight or wisdom.

We can also understand this from the teaching of the Four Noble Truths. The first truth, "All life is suffering," is a truth that can only be understood by those with concentrated minds, not distracted minds. People who are not concentrated cannot even see what is happening around them. Even if they saw it, they could not understand it because being distracted makes it impossible to see things as they are.

Just as we cannot understand what we experience in our daily lives when our minds are distracted, we cannot comprehend the first noble truth of suffering without developing concentration. It is why attention must come before insight; otherwise, understanding will be incomplete.

Sakyamuni Buddha taught that people are going through the cycle of birth, old age, and death because they do not know the Four Noble Truths. If we want to understand our experience, we need to be careful and try not to get distracted by things that cause suffering.

It is why meditating on suffering is the only correct way to contemplate it. When people practice this contemplation for a long time, they will develop insight into these truths. They will be able to give up all kinds of suffering and mental defilements such as sensual desire, ill-will, pride, and ignorance. When we have exhausted all of our mental defilements, we become liberated from them.

Chapter 5:
The Five Aggregates

Buddhism's main concepts are the five aggregates, or simpler terms, the physical and mental elements that make up each person. These are: form (rupa), sensation (vedana), perception (samjna), volition (sankhara) and consciousness (vijnana).

We will tackle the five aggregates in Buddhism, how they play a role in our spiritual journey to enlightenment, and why this concept is so crucial in Buddhist teachings on happiness. We will also examine how clinging to these aggregates can halt our progress and prevent them from causing us suffering. Finally, we will explore how emptiness (shunyata) could be considered the solution to misery and unhappiness.

Form

The form is regarded as the physical elements that make up a human being; it refers to concrete and tangible. In essence, form relates to body parts. It includes the five sensitive organs (the eyes, ears, nose, tongue, and body). The physical characteristics of our body have blood, bones, flesh, etc. It also includes our bodily fluids such as sweat, tears, etc. Form also includes anything else that belongs to our being – including our hair and nails (which are part of our body after all!). Forms can also refer to anything we consider to be out of our control, such as natural disasters, food, clothing, etc.

Form as the physical body carries a certain amount of emotional content; it is tied up with identity and self-issues to be painful. The pain of the condition lies in how we define ourselves. For example, if you hate yourself because you are overweight or have acne, this will result in suffering; some people may become anorexic because they hate their bodies, leading to pain and unhappiness. The reverse is also true; we can have a positive relationship with our bodies if we like them.

Our physical body can also be a source of pleasure. We can enjoy feeding ourselves, decorating our body, and so forth. It is just as powerful as when we are suffering; it all depends on the mind and its relation to the body.

Sensation

The sensation is defined as the awareness of the pleasant or unpleasant qualities of things. It refers to feelings you have towards something or someone. If you like a sure thing, it gives you a pleasant feeling; if you don't like something, it gives you an unpleasant feeling. If there is no particular opinion towards something, then there is no feeling at all. It does not include physical pain or pleasure, such as liking ice cream or disliking broccoli (although this may be part of goza). It instead is referring to likes and dislikes of a mental nature.

Feeling or sensations refers to either pleasant or unpleasant feelings; it is tied up with desire and attachment to life. For example, when you like the taste of the food, it is pleasant; when you dislike the taste of something (like broccoli), it is unpleasant. We all want to enjoy pleasant feelings and avoid unpleasant ones; they become a source of pain or suffering. If we fail to understand this, we can spend our lives going after pleasant feelings and failing to recognize the suffering in life; why would we need Buddhism after all when life is good! Buddhist logic would suggest that we are not good enough to be happy permanently because the basis for happiness is not stable; if it were, why would anybody need Buddhism?

Perception

Perception refers to the awareness of sensory impressions. It also includes conceptualization, recognition, understanding, etc.; it relates to mental constructs such as views or ideas.

The third aggregate refers to perception. You can perceive a particular object in many ways. We could see it as a valuable item or something of little worth. We could also see it as useful or useless; maybe you would like to own a VW Polo, but you could just be looking at it out of curiosity and so on.

When we perceive things in the world, we also value them; things are good or bad, important or unimportant, etc. The emotional content here is pretty obvious.

Volition

Volition refers to our willpower – it is the mental effort we put into something. It does not mean physical exertion; rather an action of the mind (for example, wanting to do something). Such volition can lead us away from suffering or towards it depending on what we want. For instance, we can achieve great things; our lives may become frustrating by having lousy volition.

Recollection refers to memories, so when we remember something from the past, it brings pleasure or pain. We also remember things in the present but the past; for example, we could see a person and place them from a preceding time. This aggregate can be used to refer to things like positive memories from childhood or negative ones.

Consciousness

On the other hand, consciousness refers to the necessary awareness of being; it allows us to see, hear, smell, etc.

We all have impulses – thoughts or feelings that pop into our head for no particular reason; we may have some inclinations to act on them, but we may not act upon them because we choose not to. However, the way this is represented by Buddhist philosophy is an impulse that enters our mind unannounced and leads us to act.

We can see this happening all the time; things we see or hear influence us to do something. For example, if I say I want you to come here, you may decide not to because it is too far to come; your decision comes from your free will. It is an inclination based on a decision made by free will.

We also have inclinations that we make no decision about; for example, the thought of going out for a meal pops into our heads, and we go. Our impulse also leads us to act; there is no decision involved apart from whether we want to or not.

So, it is not our free will as some like to think, but the impulses that lead us to act. It is also true for the five sense desires; they are impulses that happen inside us, and then we work on them. These impulses (kama-raga) cause us suffering because they are subject to birth and death, just like everything else in this world.

It is what Buddha was suggesting. This illusion of free will reflects our ignorance and desire to be in control of our surroundings.

We make every choice influenced by many factors, including our culture, upbringing, habits, genetics, peer pressure, etc. This conditioning leads us to believe we have free will to choose what we want for breakfast.

As individual sentient beings, we have no free will. However, we have the illusion of free will because factors outside of ourselves influence every choice we make; this illusion leads us to believe in free will.

This illusion stops us from making spiritual progress because we spend all our time pursuing things within this world and aim to control everything. We do not let go of these things because they are ours, but they are not ours: they belong to the world of illusion and delusion. We need to let go of our desire to control everything; this is true happiness.

Five Aggregates and Happiness in Buddhism

In Buddhism, there are two types of happiness: worldly happiness and spiritual happiness. Spiritual happiness is sometimes also referred to as nirvana, but they are essentially the same. To understand what these two types of Buddhism happiness are, we first have to explain what unhappiness in general is, both in a worldly sense and spiritually.

The Buddhist view on unhappiness occurs when one has a negative outlook on the world or life in general. It is commonly thought that to be happy, and one has to have a positive outlook; this is the opposite of how Buddhism sees things. In Buddhism, happiness is not contingent upon having a positive outlook.

In the third century, BC Bodhidharma said, "If you want happiness, practice sorrow; if you want joy, practice zealousness," which implies that we need to experience suffering to achieve true happiness. In Buddhism, satisfaction is about letting go of the negative things that plague us in life. It is also about letting go of our desires and our greed. As long as we cling to such things, we will never experience true spiritual happiness. This clinging on to negative things causes us suffering.

If you look at each aggregate's meaning, you will notice that they all have emotional content; each total is tied up with certain emotions, both pleasurable and painful (but mainly painful).

The Five Aggregates and Goza

Briefly, we shall now show how the five aggregates relate to goza in Buddhism. The five aggregates are also referred to as our body, mind, and speech, which are the external aspects of our existence, while vedana, sañña, and sankhara are our inner feelings which is what we have been looking for so far. Goza refers to that which stands on its own and is not tied up with anything – it is called dukkha-samuccheda-Durham (the cessation of the suffering that comes from despair). So, we can see that the five aggregates are tied up with grief and are a source of pain; they are also the basis for craving, leading us to experience more suffering. They are also what binds us to this world; they are our attachments. As long as we have these attachments, we cannot achieve spiritual happiness, which is what Buddhism is all about – it is meant to liberate us from such things.

Concentration

Meditation is the key to improving your concentration, so take the time to practice it each day. Start with simple meditation exercises, such as sitting and breathing meditations. Once you become accustomed to them, you can move on to deeper levels, such as those that enable you to reduce physical pain and emotional trauma.

To sit and meditate, you can choose to use a seated stance on a cushion on the floor where your legs are bent at the knees and crossed at the ankles. It is hard for people new to meditation to take up the more traditional lotus position at first, and this position, provided your back is straight, is a good position for meditation. Your hands can be cupped with your palms facing upward and your thumbs touching. If you use a cushion for meditation, it's an excellent idea to sway from left to right and back again to ensure that your body is grounded and comfortable before starting the breathing exercises. When you begin to meditate, make sure that you are not busy or free from distractions.

Chapter 6:
Karma

What is Karma?

Strictly speaking, the meaning of Karma refers to any action, intent, and deed by a being. It summarizes the spiritual tenet of cause and effect, wherein the actions and intentions help shape the future of that being.

In a general sense, having good intentions and doing good deeds strengthen good Karma and promote the possibility of happiness in the future. On the other hand, having lousy intent and doing evil deeds can lead to bad Karma and, hence, the chance of experiencing pain and suffering.

In traditional Buddhism, Karma specifically refers to action based on the being's intentions. Such intentions would then determine the being's cycle of rebirth. The word used to describe the "effect" of Karma is karmaphala. You can think of Karma as the seed and karmaphalaas as the fruit of that seed.

For now, let us define it as the cycle of birth and death within the six realms of the mundane world, driven by ignorance, desire, and hatred.

Laws of Karma According to Buddhism

The literal meaning of Karma is to do, to make, or to cause. It comes from "kárman" in Sanskrit, to do. The common idea is that it's synonymous with cause and effect; you're doing something, and then you're reaping the consequences. It's translated in this way under Hinduism and other Eastern cultures. It's the catalyst that triggers the kind of life you have nowadays. If someone goes through struggles, it is because they are meant to purge past life actions.

Though initially is recording the sense of Karma was Hinduism, the religion, its root, is currently in Buddhism. Both agree that the natural laws of cause and effect are sufficient to explain how Karma works; if you do good deeds, you get the gain in this or the next life.

According to Hinduism's latest writings, Karma can be created in four ways: feelings, words, acts motivated by others, and oneself. Buddhism contemplates another theory of the nature of the cause and effect of Karma, which also aligns with this, only with five categories: impact of our behavior, seasonal changes, instincts of nature, rules of inheritance and will consist of mind.

Jainism is an exciting alternative to Karma. Karma is represented under this theory by particles that vibrate according to the mind, body, and speech. The present lives are the product of Karma and our present-day soul or consciousness. There is no higher outside entity that manages the concept of cause and effect.

Buddhism is a philosophy and religion made up of practical teachings, such as meditation, which aims to induce a transformation within those who practice it. To reach a state of Enlightenment encourages the creation of wisdom, knowledge, and kindness.

Existence is viewed in Buddhism as a constant state of transition. The prerequisite for us to take advantage of these changes is creating discipline in our minds. It would concentrate on favorable conditions, such as concentration and calmness.

The course aims to develop the emotions linked to understanding, happiness, and love. Therefore, all spiritual growth for Buddhism is materialized and complemented by social work, ethics, and philosophy research.

The Twelve Karma Rules

Similar to Buddhism, these are the 12 rules of Karma:

The great law: this law in the sentence "we reap what we sow" can be summed up. It is called the law of cause and effect: what we give to the world is what the world gives us back, but if it is anything negative, it will be multiplied by ten to return to us. If we give love, we receive love, but we get anger multiplied by ten if we give hate.

The rule of creation: we have to be part of life. We are part of the universe, and with it, we form a unity. Everything we see around us is a testament to our distant history. Create the lifelong options you want.

Humility law: that which we fail to recognize will continue to happen to us. If we can see only the negative aspects of others, we will be stopped at a lower level of existence. When, on the contrary, we humbly embrace what is happening to us, we will go up to a higher degree.

Growth law: wherever we go, here is where we are going to be. We have to continue and grow in our faith in the face of events, places, and men, and not what is around us. When we change our inside, we change our life.

Responsibility law: it is because there is something terrible about us that happens to us. Our reflex is about the surroundings. And we have to face our life circumstances responsibly.

The law of connection: all we do is connected to the world, however trivial it might seem. The first step leads to the last, and both are equally necessary as they are required to achieve our goals together. It interconnects current, future, and history.

Focus law: Two things cannot be thought about simultaneously. We went up slowly, one at a time. We cannot lose sight of our ambitions because fear and rage take hold of us at those moments.

Law of giving and hospitality: if you dream of anything that may be real, then the time will come when you will be able to prove it is. We must learn to offer and bring all that has been learned into action.

The rule of the here and now: being trapped in the past makes loving the present difficult. Repetitive thoughts, poor habits, and unfulfilled dreams make it difficult for us to move forward and renew our spirit.

Law of change: History must repeat itself until the lessons we need to learn are assimilated. When a troublesome circumstance presents itself many times, we must gain some information from it. We must map our course and follow it.

Patience and Reward Law: Rewards are the product of earlier actions. Hence more outstanding commitment, more significant effort leads to more gratifications. It is a patient and persevering work that bears fruit. We will learn to enjoy our role in the world; our efforts will be honored at the right moment.

Essential and motivating law: the importance of our triumphs and mistakes depends on the purpose, and the time we expend to achieve the goal. We contribute to a universe personally, and so our acts cannot be mediocre: we have to bring all our hearts into what we do.

Karma as a Process

According to the Buddha, Karma is not an all-around determinant but rather a part of the factors that affect the future, with other factors being detailed and about the nature of the being. It moves in a fluid and dynamic way rather than in a mechanical, linear manner. Not all factors in the present can be attributed to Karma.

Be careful not to define Karma as "fate" or "foreordination." Karma is not some form of divine judgment imposed on beings that did good or bad things. Instead, it is the natural result of the process. In other words, doing a good deed would not automatically entitle you to a future of happiness, and vice versa. After all, while specific experiences in your life are due to your past actions, how you respond is not yet determined. Of course, such responses to circumstances would then lead to their consequences in the future.

Karma as Energy

All beings continuously change due to Karma. For every thought, action, and word being produced, a kind of energy is released in different directions into the universe. These energies can influence and change all other beings, including the being that sends the power.

Chapter 7:
Rebirth, The Effects of Karma on the Next Life

What is Rebirth?

Karma begets Karma: this is the essence of rebirth. Rebirth refers to the infinity of karmic tendencies. Thus, if you have good karmic tendencies, they will bring forth new good karmic tendencies. Unless you disrupt it by evil Karma, this process of good karmic tendencies will continue ad infinitum, and you will contribute to the better being of this world and yourself.

Understanding Rebirth

Death is but an impermanent end to an impermanent existence. Through powerful meditation, one can recall one's past lives. If you possess this ability, you'll be able to put your present life into a meaningful perspective.

Karma and reincarnation provide us with a plausible explanation for inequality. It shows why some men are born rich while others are born poor, why some babies are healthy while others are disabled. For some, this may be a pretty hard pill to swallow.

The belief in the cycle of rebirth is present in most of the major Indian religions, and it is most commonly called "samsara," which means "wandering." It is also one of Hinduism's core concepts, but Buddhism takes a somewhat different approach to this cycle's position. While Hinduism focuses much of its philosophy on the "atman," or soul, as the core of our being reincarnated repeatedly in samsara, Buddhism rejects the idea of soul or self altogether. The belief that we possess no soul and that self is an illusion of one of the Three Marks of Existence, which we will cover in more detail soon. All things considered, although Buddhists view samsara as a painful cycle of suffering, it's important to note that each lifetime, no matter how difficult, isn't damnation.

The condition you have been born in reflects the lesson you need to learn in this lifetime. For instance, a person may be born rich because he needs to know the value of generosity. Alternatively, a person may be born poor because he needs to learn the value of hard work.

A common question asked by skeptics is: if our souls never indeed die and if we are continually reborn in each lifetime, how does that explain that the world is more populated today than it was decades ago?

The human realm is but one of many other domains. When we pass on, we may end up in other realms. There are heavenly realms and lower realms. There are animal realms and ghostly realms. Likewise, beings from other domains may also be reborn into the human realm. Simply put, you could've been dwelling in another realm before you were reborn here in your present life. By understanding that we continuously come and go between these various realms, we gain more profound respect and empathy for other beings.

To be exact, most Buddhist teachings explain six realms of existence into which sentient beings are spawned. Those are the three higher realms of gods, demigods, humans, and three lower realms of animals, hungry ghosts, hell, or hell-beings. Sometimes, the kingdoms are viewed as only five, with the empires of gods and demigods being the same, which would make the human realm the second highest one.

Without reaching Nirvana or Buddhahood, being reborn into the realm of gods is the next best outcome one can hope for, resulting from the accumulation of perfect Karma. There is one catch associated with this realm, though, which is precisely the fact that it is a heavenly environment. Namely, it is said that the joy, luxury, and ease of life in this realm pose a problem in that a person is prone to getting too attached, which constitutes terrible Karma, of course. Therefore, if one who spawns into the godly realm is not careful and neglects their spirituality, it's quite likely that the next life will land him or her in a lower realm.

As for our human realm, even though it is primarily plagued by suffering and misfortune, it is still considered a reasonably fortunate outcome of one's karmic performance. Humans possess higher sentience and thus much freer will and independence of thought than other animals, which puts us in a position of ample opportunity to better our Karma. It is said that animals suffer immensely due to them being ruled by raw instincts that they can't control.

Of course, the last two realms are the harshest. Those born into the realm of hungry ghosts will find themselves as creatures of great craving, hunger, and thirst. The fact that they are reduced to existing as subtle, invisible beings is also said to cause much suffering. That still doesn't compare to the hellish realm reserved for those that have accumulated significant evil Karma. There are many descriptions of this realm across various traditions and texts, including multiple levels of scorching or freezing areas, realms of torture and great pain, and others.

You may be wondering how one gets out of these realms, mainly since there is a lack of awareness and free will to conduct good Karma. In essence, the demerit that one acquires through terrible Karma runs a specific course and eventually is depleted. According to one's degree of wrongdoing, particular lengths of time and punishment in hellish realms will be dished out to individuals. Remember, nothing in Buddhism is forever, and everyone can end their cycle of suffering.

Sooner or later, one will move up the bar ever so slightly and is presented with a chance to do better. Technically, one can be stuck in the lower realms indefinitely, but that will always be up to them personally. And while many of the rebirths into the human realm can be quite painful and tough on people, they should never forget that, unlike animals, they can commit to their karmic outcome truly and significantly accelerate the accumulation of good Karma.

You might be wondering if that lack of free will in the lower realms means that Karma can't get worse, in addition to there being no way to improve it. In general, this would be a correct assumption due to that fundamental issue of free will. To put it simply, there exist multiple realms that are below and are worse than the human one primarily to account for various levels of evil Karma that people acquire, not because animals or hungry ghosts can do evil deeds and get themselves reborn into an even lower realm. Buddhists generally believe that animals and other inferior creatures are incapable of really doing any wrong, just as they are incapable of doing good. When animals kill, they do so out of necessity and a need for food or basic survival, not because they like it or following an ideology. Therefore, all there is for animals and other lower beings to do is live out their lives and wait for their bad Karma to run out.

It is life in one of the higher, conscious realms that determine how lowly you will be reborn, based on how evil your Karma is. Animals generally can't find themselves reborn into the realms of hungry ghosts or hell. Instead, they can either remain in their domain or move up after they die.

About the Tibetan Book of the Dead

Those who have heard a few things about Buddhism in passing may have, at some point, also heard of something that is commonly referred to as the "Tibetan Book of the Dead." This piece of literature is intimately concerned with the concept of rebirth and death itself, but it's not quite as eerie as it first sounds.

The way that this book came to be in its current form in the West is quite a long story, but far more critical are its origins and subject matter. With all its gradual additions, reinterpretations, adaptations, and revisions, this "book" is rooted in the old literature of Bardo Thodol, meaning "The Great Liberation through Hearing in the Intermediate State." Various research efforts have uncovered that Bardo Thodol was most likely authored in the 8th century, after which it was buried at some point until being unearthed and revealed to the world by Karma Lingpa, a 14th-century man who is believed to have been a Nyingma teacher.

Chapter 8:
How to Practice Buddhism

Practices of Buddhism

Buddhism's primary emphasis is on overcoming our shortcomings and fully enhancing our positive potential. Limitations include a lack of clarity and an emotional imbalance that confuses us about life. Consequently, we conduct ourselves compulsively, motivated by troubling emotions like frustration, greed, and naivety. Our positive potentials include our ability to communicate, understand reality, empathize with others, and better ourselves.

The Fourteenth Dalai Lama

We all care about our physical hygiene, but taking care of our mental state is just as critical. We need to remember the antidotes to our upsetting state of mind, remember to apply them when necessary, and remember to retain them.

To remember all the antidotes, you must:

Learn what they are.

Contemplate them until we understand them correctly, knowing how to apply them, and being convinced that they will work.

Practice applying them in meditation to become familiar with them.

Buddhist Practice, Preliminaries, and Rites

Medicine Buddha: The mantra and the medicine Buddha image are perfect for your health and that of others, for your mind in short. Meditate on the Medicine Buddha idea, and if you accompany it with a bowl, the result is perfect.

The Third Ray, Active Intelligence, connects with the fifth Center. It is recited by visualizing the Blue Medicine Buddha, or instead, a sphere of blue light, which in essence represents the Medicine Buddha.

They can be visualized on the forehead or crown. In reciting the mantra, the reciter visualizes rays of light and nectar emanating from the sphere of light, penetrating the head's peak and clearing all diseases, tensions, and blockages.

With the same procedure, healing water can be obtained, increasing the power of medications and medical treatments. It helps recite the mantra while visualizing the Medicine Buddha pouring over the medicine we are taking, imagining that the prescription is filled with the mixture of Buddha's light energy.

Gong Bath: When we listen to the Gong's sound, deep relaxation is created—freeing us from the torrent of thoughts that our mind generates. During a Gong Bath, you will experience sensations inside and outside the body. The sound caresses you as if it were a wave. At the cellular level, vibration also works by harmonizing all body cells by the physical principle of sound resonance. A Gong Bath is an experience that will never leave you indifferent. Let yourself go, flow like water, and let the sound guide you.

Dalai Lama Guru Yoga: Through the practice of Guru Yoga, we are inspired by the example of the spiritual master. By placing ourselves under his guidance, we progressively reveal our mind's essential nature, developing and training its positive qualities. Guru Yoga is essential in Vajrayana Buddhism because, on this path, achievements depend on the purity of commitment (Samaya) and how we perceive and relate to the teacher.

The Dalai Lama himself wrote the Dalai Lama's Inseparability Guru Yoga Practice with Avalokitesvara (Compassionate Buddha). It contained a meditation on Avalokitesvara and a complete meditation on the gradual path to enlightenment.

Shabab Duchen: Shabab Düchen is one of the four most crucial Buddhist tradition celebrations: prayer and virtuous actions. Shabab Düchen is the celebration of the Buddha's descent from the paradise of Tushita to give Dharma teachings to his mother, Queen Mayadevi. It is part of the Tibetan Buddhist tradition to dedicate this day to prayer and virtuous actions. In this celebration, it is believed that the or merits of all right actions are multiplied by 10 million times, and adverse actions also give this same multiplier effect.

Lama Chöpa: This Buddhist ceremony is observed during the "days of Tsog" in the Tibetan calendar. It is an indispensable practice for Vajrayana practitioners. Guru Yoga is the root of the spiritual path and the basis for reaching all spiritual realizations. Compiled by the First Panchen Lama, the fundamental pillar of this practice is devotion to the teacher. Still, it also contains all the essential instructions of the stages of the path and those related to the locations of generation consummation of the Supreme Tantra.

Offering the Tsog is very important to keep commitments and avoid obstacles, as we place ourselves under the care of dakas and dakinis, who grant us realizations. Furthermore, our health, merits, and joy increase by doing this practice. As it is an offering ritual, you must attend it with offerings of flowers, food, or drink.

Initiations: A tantric initiation is a power transmission ceremony that activates our Buddha-nature's evolutionary factors, stimulating them further. Receiving initiation requires a fully trained tantric master and prepared and receptive, and that our participation is active in the process. Initiations are allusive to a specific tantric entity: Vajra sattva, Chenrezig, Tara, Manjushri. They are usually accompanied by teachings related to said entities' qualities, and receiving them implies the teacher's authorization and blessing to perform them independently. Many of them indicate a firm commitment on our part, both philosophical and daily practice.

Vajra Sattva Practice: one Friday a month at 6:30 p.m.

Doing the Vajra Sattva practice and reciting the 100-syllable mantra 100,000 times purifies negativities, provided it is done correctly, with all factors complete. If the recitation is done without the four elements, we cannot filter the negativities in their entirety. However, if the meditation and recitation of Vajra Sattva are appropriately done, with the four opposing powers, and we recite the mantra 100,000 times, all negativities are purified. Repeating the mantra 21 times every day prevents negativity from increasing.

Chod Practice: one Friday a month at 7:00 p.m.

The practice of Chöd is part of the cultural heritage of Tibetan Buddhism. The traditional approach of Chöd cuts self-esteem, and clinging to a real existence of the "I" creates the conditions under which the conventional bodhicitta mind can develop, which holds others as dearer than oneself, and the Ultimate Bodhicitta mind, which sees reality as it is.

By cutting out our habitual selfish patterns of thought and behavior, we allow the natural openness, clarity, and sensitivity of the mind to manifest. Strong and spontaneous compassion arises when we experience our union with the universe and with all sentient beings that inhabit it.

With this practice, we simultaneously train the body, speech, and Mind through meditation, visualization, sound, and rhythm. Like all tantric practices, Chöd can only be performed after receiving the lineage's initiation and instructions by a fully qualified master. The family to which the Chöd practice that we follow in our Center belongs to the Wensa Tradition's Gelugpa lineage.

It is also known as the Chöd practice of Padampa Sangye and belongs to the Manjushri collection. Chöd was a private practice of Lama Tsongkhapa. The great master Gyelwa Ensapa Losang Dondrup, the first Panchen Rinpoche, received the Lama Tsongkhapa lineage initiation, which had been transmitted continuously until it reached him.

Praises at 21 Taras: Wednesdays at 7:00 p.m.

Tara is a Buddha with a feminine aspect, who, out of great compassion, promised to lead to Enlightenment in a single lifetime, all the beings who entrusted themselves to her. The praise of the twenty-one forms of Tara was composed by the Buddha himself and is a widespread practice in all Tibetan Buddhism schools. Its recitation brings great because being a Sutra, the very words of Buddha,

This practice is very suitable to eliminate obstacles, fears, diseases, achieve prosperity, well-being, abundance, and happiness. Given the current circumstances, it is necessary to create the causes for temporary and ultimate well-being, both for ourselves and our environment: family, friends, colleagues, fellow citizens, compatriots, and all sentient beings in general. To alleviate hunger and disease, wars, injustice, and to ensure that all beings enjoy the qualities of enlightenment. It is delicious to recite the praise at 21 Taras as often as possible.

Prostrations: Tuesdays at 7:00 p.m.

The prostrations are a vital act of respect towards the Buddha, the Dharma, and the Sangha, which constitute the Three Jewels. They are also an antidote to pride, and it is a form of accumulation of merit and purification of negativities. There are two types of physical prostrations, short (5 points) and long. The prostrations performed in this practice are the long ones. For most Buddhists, there are at least three situations in which we must prostrate ourselves unless we go on a pilgrimage trip or do certain specific practices:

When entering a gompa: It is a sign of respect for performing three prostrations before the main altar. Also, when you are going to leave until another day.

In the presence of the teacher: When you wait for the lama to enter to offer to teach or lead a puja, you have to wait for him to sit on his throne. Then three short prostrations are done before sitting down, and they are repeated when the lama gets up to leave.

When placing and removing the altar: Immediately after setting up the altar and just before beginning to remove it, three prostrations should be made at a time.

The mantra that is usually recited when doing prostrations is Om Namo Manjushriye, Namo Sushriye, Namo Utama Shriye Soha. What it means: I pay homage to the impeccable Buddha Mind, I pay tribute to the noble and glorious Dharma, and I pay homage to the Glorious Order (Sangha).

The prostrations to the Thirty-Five Buddhas of Confession are a powerful method if carried out as the first activity in the morning, to purify any negativity created during the night, and as the last thing in the day, to purify negativities. In which we may have incurred during the day. Through this practice, the mind, speech, and body participate in the purification process.

How to practice Buddhism

Unlike any other spiritual philosophy, Buddhism, neither better nor worse, but unique, teaching less about the value of divine deities and rules and more about a way of life that can change our inner world and, ultimately, the world around us. This practice reverts to what is now known as Nepal and started 2600 years ago. While there are many schools within Buddhism today, there is a common understanding that all Buddhists share.

Yet why is it that people practice Buddhism? While there are several explanations, one of the core concepts is in his belief that all beings are experiencing the essential wear and tear of birth, maturity, illness, and death, so we must go beyond this normal wear and tear, life, and death.

Chapter 9:
Guidelines for Practicing Buddhism

Throughout the centuries, Buddhist practices have been transforming based on the people who continue to uphold them. How the methods are adopted is based on the culture of different societies. Yet, one thing remains the same: the core values of Buddhism are preserved. Such virtues are being strong-willed, generous, kind, and selfless are universally accepted and timeless.

You will learn how they can help you to become stress- and anxiety-free at the least, and how they can help you stay motivated as you follow the Noble Eightfold Path.

Mindfulness Meditation

When you talk about Buddhism, you cannot avoid mentioning the concept of meditation. It is the core of the practice. Additionally, scientific studies can attest to its mental and physical gain. Meditation is a generally accepted and widely recommended way to reduce stress in everyday life, improve cognitive and emotional intelligence, and increase positive thinking.

Theravada Buddhism Meditation:

- Anapanasati

- Satipatthana

- Metta

- Kammatthana

- Samatha

- Vipassana

- Mahasati

- Dhammakaya

Vajrayana and Tibetan Buddhism Meditation

- Ngondro

- Tonglen

- Phowa

- Chod

- Mahamudra

- Dzogchen

- The Four Immeasurables

- Tantra

Zen Buddhism Meditation

- Shikantaza (sitting meditation)

- Zazen

- Koan

- Suizen

Chanting and Mantras

Another common practice in Buddhism is chanting. Buddhist monks in different parts of East and Southeast Asia practice regularly chanting to improve their concentration and reflect deeply on Buddhist concepts. Buddhists modernists use phrases in their spoken language to create mantras that help them sink deeper into their meditative state as well.

You may be familiar with the "Om," a sacred mantra that Buddhists chant at the start of all mantras. According to ancient Hindu texts, Om is the eternal sound in the past, present, and future. It embodies birth, life, and death, and it is used and heard every day. Interestingly, it is said that by chanting "Om," the vibrations it causes helps relax the body and mind.

There are also centers whose gurus give individual chants to students based upon the year, time, and place of birth, and these are personal to the student. Chanting is found useful in many ways because it allows the student to concentrate on a given thing rather than allowing the mind to wander. Although this was not the specific purpose of mantras, it helps to cut out unnecessary thought processes that help the student meditate more successfully. It also allows the student to breathe since some mantras are used in rhythm with the breathing and help the student breathe and chant the mantra on the outward breath.

Vegetarian or Vegan Lifestyle

While it must be noted that the First Buddha himself never mentioned anything against the consumption of meat, many Buddhists choose to live the vegetarian or vegan lifestyle. Therefore, by harming another being, one is breaking the self as well.

Some Buddhists who choose to eat meat do so only out of necessity. For instance, those living in cold climates can only survive on a diet rich in fat and protein. In such cases, the Buddhists would then choose only the meat of ethically raised animals. In other words, the animals lived a full and relatively happy and free life and were slaughtered most humanely and painlessly for their meat.

Ultimately, the decision to choose your diet rests in your hands, as the Buddha himself explained. Of course, no one is exempted from eating meat's karmic results, mostly if the living being was slaughtered specifically for you. It is worthy of note since Buddhist monks are often given food, and there is a story about a Buddhist monk who was extremely hungry. He was given a chicken plate and looked forward to eating it until he was told that the chicken had been slaughtered specifically for him. In this case, he was not permitted to eat it since this goes against Buddhist belief, and he was considered the cause of the killing.

As you can see, many – if not all – of Buddhism practices can easily be incorporated into the modern lifestyle. It is up to you how you perceive and practice these rituals each day. After all, it is only through experience that you can truly witness the gain of these practices.

Would it surprise you to know that Buddhism is not a religion? At least, not in a sense wherein it is an institution that dictates how one should believe in divine power. Many people make that mistake and avoid Buddhism because they think it contrary to their church's teachings. However, you can practice Buddhism in conjunction with your personal belief and religion or complement it.

Your real self is what can be understood to travel from life to life during reincarnation. In different belief systems, these are given names, such as the soul, though what name you give it isn't vital. It is merely crucial that you recognize that these two parts of you exist and that, if you are unhappy in your life, the harmony or balance is missing, and that's where Buddhism helps you to align these values so that both parts of you are in connection with each other.

Each living being has the opportunity to become enlightened in each life they live. There is no set course or prewritten script for your life. However, things get interesting here because when you follow Buddhism's path, you do not have an "end goal." It is a paradox for one to declare that they are going to practice Buddhism to reach enlightenment.

At this point, you must be eager to learn the different teachings of the Buddha. Keep in mind that the Buddha's teachings are vast to such an extent that they grew into many Buddhism kinds. These teachings can bring wisdom to anyone, whether seeking to find their real self through enlightenment or those that wish to understand the world around them a little bit better. These teachings are for the young and old alike, regardless of religion, status, gender, or heritage.

You have to discern the truth for yourself because your truth will not be everyone else's. With the constant changes that happen throughout life, the Buddhist belief encourages that you embrace the moment and are ever-present in it. For westerners, this is always a little difficult since we are always striving to better ourselves, although sometimes the betterment that we seek is detrimental. If you were to talk to Tibetans, they do not find merit in people trying to prove that they are better than others. Boasting is not part of the Buddhist way of life, which contrasts with life in a modern society that encourages competition and heroics with very little to do with betterment from a Buddhist perspective.

Siddhartha Gautama's idea was to encourage people to understand that their actions dictate the outcome of different life stages. It is always something that westerners find hard to understand. However, when you see how Buddhist philosophy includes other elements, you will see that the whole picture of your life has been covered and that there are actions you can take to increase your awareness and sense of happiness. Our current Dalai Lama was once asked what surprised him the most about humankind, and his answer will give you something to think about, which relates to modern times and which you can probably identify with.

Chapter 10:
The Roots of Evil

The following are the Three Poisons that every Buddhist must strive to avoid. They are regarded as the primary source of evil manifested through our actions, speech, and thoughts. They are considered as blocks to positive Karma.

Greed

It includes an insatiable desire for:

- Riches
- Fame
- Sex
- Sleep
- Overcome greed by performing simple acts of generosity.

Anger

Practice calmness and patience. Do not allow anger to dictate your actions. Once you do, you will enable it to dictate your Karma and dictate your future life quality.

Ignorance

As a Buddhist, you are urged to embrace the truth. Let go of prejudices. Stop clinging to delusions. Use your intellect and your senses to carry out observations in an objective manner.

Think of life as a wheel that turns round and round. Depending on your past life deeds, you may be born on top or at the bottom. And so, this goes on and on until you are finally able to experience the awakening. The purpose of reincarnation is to give you a chance to escape the ever-turning wheel of life eventually. It is done by achieving enlightenment. Accordingly, to do this means you must first successfully become free of the Three Poisons.

Remember to also apply the wheel metaphor to this very life and not just the excellent rebirth cycle. The suffering, temptation, and hardship that, as you have learned, come into every life are things that oscillate a great deal. Since both sorrow and happiness are subject to the doctrine of impermanence, the very life that you are traversing now is certainly also reminiscent of a great wheel, although not as great as the one of Samsara. Nonetheless, Anicca will always have you alternating between the top and bottom of the revolution, between the good times and bad, health and sickness. As long as you do, you will always end up better than you started, no matter how far you manage to get.

Radical Teachings

Some of Zen's traditional stories describe masters using unorthodox education methods, and many practitioners today tend to interpret these stories overly literally.

For example, many are outraged when they hear stories like that of Master Linji, the founder of the Rinzai school, who said, "If you find the Buddha, kill the Buddha. If you find a Patriarch, kill the patriarch." A contemporary master, Seung Sahn, also teaches his students that we all need to kill three things: kill our parents, kill the Buddha, and kill our teacher (in this case, Seung Shan himself). However, neither Linji nor Seung Sahn was speaking literally. They wanted to say that we need to "kill" our attachment to outside teachers and things.

When visiting temples or Zen practice centers, beginners who have read many of these stories and expect to find iconoclastic teachers are often surprised by the conservative and formal nature of practices.

Zen and Other Religions

Since the mid-twentieth century, Zen has been open to interreligious dialogue, having appeared in countless meetings and conferences worldwide. In Zen temples and centers of practice worldwide, it is common for many non-Buddhists to attend activities and practice zazen. This practice is generally well accepted by teachers since Buddhism is a religion of tolerance that sees other religions as valid spiritual paths and is open to anyone who only wants to meditate without any religious affiliation.

In some schools, Sanbo Kyodan, the acceptance of practitioners of other religions is so high that a practitioner can receive the Dharma transmission and become a teacher without needing to leave their faith.

Statements like that of the former Pope, who called the Dalai Lama "godless," naturally had a considerable and (of course) adverse effect on the population's masses.

The Illumination

In Zen, enlightenment is generally called Satori or kensho. The kensho is the initial glimpse, so to speak, of the true nature of reality and of itself. It's a shallow form of enlightenment. On the other hand, Satori is a more profound and more lasting experience in which the practitioner has an intense experience of Buddha's Nature and sees his "original face."

But it is not a visionary experience. Although some people suppose that enlightenment experience should lead those who experience it to universes of intense light or something worth it, the testimony of Zen masters contradicts this hypothesis. When asked about how his life was before and how he stayed after Satori, a modern Zen master replied, "Now my garden looks more colorful." In enlightenment, the practitioner is not distracted.

Another common assumption is that when being enlightened, the flow of thoughts stops. The practitioner stands as a polished mirror, reflecting the actual reality without ideas that will hinder it. On the contrary, dreams do not stay - what happens is that the practitioner gives them up, lets them go, forgets them, and forgets himself. When the Fifth Patriarch, Hongren (in Japanese, Damian Konin, 601-647), decided to choose who would succeed him, he proposed to his disciples that they try to capture Zen's essence in a poem; the author of the best poem would be his successor. When they received the news, the monks knew who the winner was: Shenxiu, Hongren's oldest student. No one bothered to compete with him. They just waited, and Shexiu wrote his poem and hung it on the wall:

"This body is the Bodhi tree.

The soul is like a bright mirror.

Take care that it is always clean,

leaving no dust accumulates on it."

All the monks liked it. Surely Hongren would enjoy it too. However, the next day there was another poem hanging by the side, which someone had preached during the night:

"Bodhi is not like a tree.

The bright mirror shines nowhere:

If there is nothing from the beginning,

Where does dust accumulate?"

The monks were amazed. Who would have written that? After a while, they discovered: the author of the poem was Huineng, the monastery cooks. And realizing his achievement, it was to him that Hongren extended his cloak and his bowl, making Huineng the Sixth Patriarch.

Like all Buddhist schools, Zen sends its roots back to Indian Buddhism. The word Zen comes from the Sanskrit term dhyana, which denotes the typical meditative practice state. In China, this term was transliterated as channa and soon reduced to its shorter form. From there, it translated to Korean and finally to Japanese as Zen.

According to traditional accounts, the Zen practice style was taken from India to China by the Indian monk Bodhidharma (in Japanese, Daruma), circa AD 520. Although modern scholars have questioned this account's origin and authenticity, Bodhidharma's story (or legend) is the fundamental metaphor of Zen on the core of its practice.

In Second Counts Registration Lamp Transmission, one of Zen's oldest texts, Bodhidharma, went to China. Due to his wise fame, the Liang Dynasty's territory was immediately summoned to the famous Emperor Wu-ti court. The emperor, who had broadly supported Buddhism in China, asked Bodhidharma about the merit he had gained by supporting Buddhism, hoping that this merit would ensure him a good life in his next incarnation. Bodhidharma replied, "No merit." The emperor, enraged, then asked, "Who is this that is before me?" (in present-day language, something like "Who do you think you are?") Bodhidharma replied, "I do not know." Dazed, the emperor concluded that Bodhidharma must be mad and expelled him from the court. One of the ministers then asked the emperor: "Your Imperial Majesty knows who this person is?" The emperor said he did not know. The Minister said, "He is the Bodhisattva of Compassion, bearer of the Seal of the Buddha's Heart." "Full of regret, the emperor wanted to call Bodhidharma back, but the Minister warned that he would not come back even if all the Chinese went to pick him up. Other people, however, we're intrigued by his response and followed him to the cave where he had gone to live. They became his disciples and discovered that Bodhidharma was the spiritual heir of Mahakashyapa, one of Buddha's great disciples.

According to traditional teachings, Bodhidharma could not answer because his true nature and the true nature of all things were beyond discursive knowledge, definition, and words. It is to this direct experience of reality that Zen aspires.

Mahakashyapa, of whom Bodhidharma was a spiritual heir and successor, had himself this experience and was enlightened. According to the sutras, Mahakashyapa was Buddha's only disciple to understand his Lotus Speech, in which Buddha, without saying anything, simply raised a flower. It was an immediate reality, beyond words.

After training his disciples for many years, Bodhidharma died, leaving his student Huike (Japanese, Daiso Eka). Huike was the second Patriarch of Zen and went through a succession line of which little is known until arriving at Huineng (in Japanese, DaikanEno, 638-713), the sixth and last Patriarch. Huineng, one of the greatest masters of Zen history, participated in a famous dispute when his master succeeded: a group of monks refused to accept him as patriarch and proposed another practitioner, Shenxiu, in his place. Huineng was forced to flee to a temple in southern China under threat, but in the end, supported by most of the monks, she was recognized as a patriarch.

A few decades later, however, the feud was resurrected. A group of monks, claiming to be Shenxiu's successor, faced another group, the Southern School, which presented itself as Huineng's successor. After heated debates, the Southern School eventually prevailed, and its rivals disappeared. The records of this dispute are the earliest historical records of the Zen school we have today.

Later, Korean monks went to China to study the practices of the Bodhidharma school. When they arrived, what they found was a school that had already developed its own identity with strong Taoism influences, formerly known by Chan's name. Over time, Chan eventually settled in Korea, where he received the name Seon.

Similarly, monks came from other Asian countries to study Chan, and the school spread to neighboring countries. In Vietnam, it was called Thien, and in Japan, it became known as Zen. These schools have grown independently throughout history, having developed their own identities and characteristics entirely different from one another.

Zazen

For Zen, experiencing reality is experiencing nirvana. To experience reality directly, one must detach oneself from words, concepts, and discourses. And to separate yourself from this, one must meditate. Therefore, Zazen ("sitting meditation") is the actual application of Zen.

Chapter 11:
Zen

Zen Buddhism is the Japanese name of a school that originated in China in the 5th century and is related to the Great Way (Mahayana). It, too, relies on explanations given by the Buddha himself to his disciples. Many Zen schools regard knowledge and conventions as useless ballast. Enlightenment should break through in a flash through self-arising insight.

Particularly well-known in the West are Zen meditations. The participants sit still for hours or ponder a paradoxical question (Japanese: Koan) to exhaust the constant flow of inner ideas. Zen Buddhism was mainly passed on in Japan.

What is Zen Buddhism?

Zen Buddhism, like any other form of Buddhism, originated from Buddha. After his enlightenment, he developed countless ways to teach his disciples to reach the experience of awakening. This time instead of talking, he raised a lotus flower with one of his hands without saying a word and just sketched a soft smile. All the disciples gathered there could see the gesture but did not realize what he wanted to convey. However, one of his chief disciples, Mahakashyapa, could understand and grasp the message that the Buddha sent beyond any word. This particular event, in which the Buddha could silently communicate something of the spirit of awakening, is considered the beginning of Zen's great tradition.

Without depending on words or letters, Zen tries to bring the practice and teaching of awakening beyond any doctrine, scripture, or conventional communication method. Zen Buddhism is a concrete and immediate way of emitting the essence of Enlightenment experience and seeing things as they are. It is pointing directly to the mind.

Zen Buddhism is a branch of late Indian Buddhism called Mahayana. The Mahayana has several philosophical backgrounds. One of the schools called Madhyamika, which emphasizes the empty nature of things from the Shunyata doctrine. Zen Buddhism likewise stresses that the mind or consciousness is identical to what he perceives, emphasizing the Mahayana philosophical school called Yogachara.

According to this doctrine, to reach the full experience of awakening, one must directly contact the nature of mind or consciousness in its most profound sense. In this way, Zen Buddhism considers the mind to be identical with reality, and this means that if we want to reach full awakening, we have to approach that which allows us to perceive it directly. We have to contact our mind directly - this is carried out through meditation.

History of Zen Buddhism

Zen or Zen-Buddhism is the Japanese name of the Ch'an tradition, originated in China, and associated with Buddhism's origins is the Mahayana branch, Sanskrit, "Great Vehicle," a doctrinal synthesis of the Buddha's teachings Gautama Buddha, performed by various Buddhist schools around the second century. Cultivated mainly in China, Japan, Vietnam, and Korea. Zen's essential practice in the Japanese and monastic version is Zazen, a type of contemplative meditation that aims to bring the practitioner to the "direct experience of reality."

In Japanese monastic Zen, there are two main strands: Soto and Rinzai. While the Soto school places greater emphasis on silent meditation, the Rinzai school makes extensive use of koans, riddles, or charades. Zen is currently one of the most well-known and expanding Buddhist schools in the West.

According to Allan Watts, an Englishman who became famous for Zen's spread in the West from the third decade of the twentieth century, Zen's original form is no longer in China. What is closer to this original version is found in traditional Japanese art forms that have been cultivated and transmitted according to this tradition.

There are several legends within the Zen tradition, transmitted and renewed by the oral tradition and parts of Chinese and Japanese folklore that intertwine with history. Narratives of oral tradition, many of which are compiled into literary anthologies, maybe, according to different views of theorists, considered legends, folklore, and mythology literature.

Zen-Buddhism's origins have pointed to the Flower Sermon (mentioned earlier), whose earliest source comes from the 14th century. Gautama Buddha joined his disciples to a Dharma speech. When they entered, the Buddha remained utterly silent, and some thought he was tired or sick. The Buddha raised a flower silently, and several disciples tried to interpret what this meant, though none of them did adequately. One of the disciples, Mahakashyapa, silently looked at the flower and obtained a unique understanding beyond the words - prajna, or "wisdom," directly from the Mind of the Buddha. Mahakashyapa somehow understood the true inexpressible meaning of the flower, and the Buddha smiled at him, acknowledging his knowledge and said:

"I possess the pure eye of the Dharma, the wonderful mind of Nirvana, the original form of the report, the delicate Dharma portal which does not depend on words or writings but it's a special communication outside the scriptures, this I pass to Mahakashyapa."

Mahakashyapa is, by this rare gift of understanding, considered the founding patriarch by Chinese Zen, or (Ch'an). In this way, through Zen, a path was developed that focused on direct experience rather than on rational beliefs or revealed scriptures. Wisdom was passed not through words but the lineage of the direct transmission of mind to the mind or a teacher's thought to a disciple. It is commonly believed that this lineage has continued uninterrupted from the Buddha's time to the present day.

Historically this belief is debatable because of the lack of evidence to support it. According to DT Suzuki, the idea of a line of descent from Gautama Buddha is a distinctive Zen institution. He believes scholars invented it through hagiography to give legitimacy and prestige to Zen.

Philosophy and Practice of Zen Buddhism

Zen is a branch of the Mahayana Buddhist tradition and is fundamentally based on Siddhartha Gautama's teachings, the historical Buddha, and the founder of Buddhism. However, through its history, Zen also received influences from the countries' diverse cultures it has passed through.

Its formative period in China, in particular, determined much of its identity. Taoist teachings and practices exerted considerable influence on Chinese Chan. Concepts such as Huawei, the fluid nature of reality, and the "non-carved stone" can still be identified in Japanese Zen and related schools." Even the Zen tradition of "mad masters" is a continuation of the rule of Taoist masters. Another influence though minor, came from Confucianism.

Such peculiarities have led some scholars to argue that Zen is an "independent" school outside the Mahayana tradition - or even Buddhism. These positions, however, are a minority. The vast majority of scholars regard Zen as a Buddhist school within the Mahayana tradition.

All Zen schools are well-versed in Buddhist philosophy and doctrine, including the Four Noble Truths, the Noble Eightfold Path, and the parasites. However, Zen's emphasis on experiencing reality directly, in addition to ideas and words, always keeps it within the limits of tradition.

This openness enabled (and allowed) non-Buddhists to practice Zen, such as the Jesuit priest Hugo Enomiya-Lassalle, to receive the

Dharma transmission and many other non-Buddhists.

Zen Practices and Teachings

In general, Zen's teachings criticize the study of texts and the desire for worldly achievements and focus on a dedication to meditation (Zazen) to directly experience the mind and reality. However, Zen does not become a quietist doctrine - the Chinese Chan Baizhang (in Japanese, Hyakujo, 720-814), for example, devoted himself to manual work in his monastery and had as his motto a saying that remained famous among Zen practitioners: "A day without work is a day without food."

Zen has a long tradition of meditative work, from manual to refined activities such as calligraphy, ikebana, and the famous tea ceremony in addition to martial arts. Zen has always been connected. However, these practices are well-grounded in the Buddhist scriptures, especially in the Mahayana sutras composed in India and China, particularly the Huineng Platform Sutra, Heart Diamond Lankavatara Sutra, and Samantamukha Parivarta, a part of the Lotus Sutra. The significant influence of the Lankavatara Sutra, in particular, led to the formation of Zen's "mind-only" philosophy, in which consciousness itself is the only reality.

Zen is not a style of intellectual or solitary practice. Of course, temples and centers always assemble a group of practitioners (a sangha) and conduct daily activities and monthly retreats (sessions). Also, Zen is seen as a way of life, not just as a set of practices or a state of consciousness.

Zen and Meditation

Likewise, Zen is the school of Buddhism that takes reflection as a direct way to reach awakening. All schools of Buddhism also take meditation as a practice and try to achieve full awareness. However, Zen is among the different traditional schools that take meditation as the primary tool to reach this achievement.

The word Zen is of Japanese origin and is derived from Chan's Chinese name, which Mahayana Buddhism practiced in China from which Zen arose. In turn, the story Chan is a transliteration of the Sanskrit word Dhyana. The term Dhyana describes the experience of meditative absorption that occurs after an effective concentration. In the ancient discourses of the Buddha, up to eight different levels of this absorption are detailed.

They were observing our nature and awakening to Buddhahood. Buddahood happens when you reach your ultimate enlightenment. Zen considers that any person has the potential for Enlightenment and Buddhahood in his experience; this is a very particular feature of Zen Buddhism. When practitioners become involved with any aspect of their practice, be it conscious attention, compassion, or whatever they assume, that quality is already inherent in their experience. Consequently, the method consists of opening up and discovering what already exists in its condition; this makes Zen practice very positive, affirmative and allows its practitioners to progress naturally and directly. In essence, Zen affirms that we are all Buddhas, and training helps discover this fact more deeply.

A peculiarity of Buddhist ethics can be found in Zen Buddhism.

Here, the prohibition of intoxicating means is emphasized. It is related to the fact that in Zen Buddhism, the right mindfulness has a significant role. Moreover, intoxicants prevent a clear and always alert mind. Another peculiarity that only occurs in Zen Buddhism is the great importance of goodness and compassion. In Zen Buddhism, the idea of universal love is emphasized as much as the concept of charity in Christianity. That is why nonviolence, peacefulness, and love of one's enemies are sought.

Chapter 12:
Buddhism and Christianity

Buddhism and Christianity are two religions with great significance in the world. They both have beliefs, doctrines, principles, and traditions that can seem very similar at first glance. However, it is also easy to see where they differ. Buddhism is non-theistic, while Christianity holds Jesus Christ as its central figure.

When observing similarities between these two religious traditions, it is hard not to focus on the fact that both are founded on a Book, i.e., the Holy Bible for Christians and the Tripitaka for Buddhists. There are five precepts in Buddhism: not harming any sentient being, not lying or deceiving anyone, no stealing, and respect for parents and elders.

Both religions also emphasize the benefit of leading a life of self-discipline and meditation. Similarly, Christian monasticism developed to include forms like Lectio Divina, where one spends time alone in his cell reading Bible passages for contemplation.

Christianity and Buddhism have differing views on what happens after death. Christianity teaches that Jesus is the only way to salvation. Still, Buddhists believe in an "intermediate state" where beings go through a judicial process that determines if they should be reborn or not. The judgment is based on whether individuals have led a virtuous life full of merit and good behavior. Christian doctrine holds that Jesus died for sinners to free them from their sins, while Buddhist teaching holds that lives are infinite and beings reincarnate until they become enlightened.

The notion of salvation and the afterlife is reflected in many of their symbols and rituals. In Buddhism, Nirvana is the ultimate goal for each individual. It represents a state of spiritual liberation where all desires are extinguished. Nirvana is achieved when all things are understood to be non-existent, and Buddha was said to have attained Nirvana 2500 years ago before passing it on to others.

The differences between these two world religions can also be seen in their lifestyles. Buddhist monks and nuns practice celibacy, while priests in the Roman Catholic Church are allowed to marry. Christian tradition teaches that Jesus was married to Mary Magdalene and many Christians look upon Mary as an essential figure in their religion. Buddhists also take a firm stance on environmental issues and participate in activities like tree planting on a global scale.

Although there is no doubt that they are different, there is no denying that they both believe in certain fundamental principles that can be found across many other religions.

Similarities of Buddhism and Christianity

Eager for a spiritual journey into knowledge and enlightenment? Want to transcend the mundane, conventional, and superficial ways of life? Were you intrigued by the similarities between Buddhism and Christianity?

If you answered yes to any of these questions, read on! We have compiled two articles that show intriguing parallels between these well-known religions. The first article takes a comparative look at how both religions deal with telling someone that they are no longer a part of their group. Surprisingly, while they may use different methods, their overall goal is the same: To keep on saving as many people as possible by eliminating those who do not fit in with their set standards. The second article takes a comparative look at how both religions define the word "peace," ultimately concluding that peace is something you need to work towards, not an instantaneous reward.

Buddhism and Christianity both have strict requirements for those who want to join their group. However, to ensure that they are keeping only the best members, they have different ways of approaching ex-communication. Buddhism focuses on doing good deeds to keep up with the standards required for belonging to their group (Wallis).

It is referred to as "meritorious action." It was the way Buddhists dealt with ex-communication. The malaise was that "good" deeds were sometimes misconstrued and that people who completed these deeds but did not meet the requirements of belonging to the group were sometimes still granted entrance (Wallis). Therefore, they found a new way to keep up with their standards by doing away with merit and instead focusing on being the right person. It is called the Eightfold Path on Buddha's Wheel of Dharma.

Christianity uses the church community as its primary tool in ex-communication. Those who are kicked out or deny entrance are typically people who have committed one of a few sins. These sins are murder, sexual immorality, theft, and blasphemy (Lowder). The reasoning behind these few serious sins is that they are acts that go against the Ten Commandments. Since Christianity believes all humans are sinners, they think it is necessary to find a scapegoat to explain the reason for their wrongdoings. This scapegoat is known as Satan or Lucifer (Lowder). "The idea of a scapegoat giving up his soul to has been with the Christian Church since its beginning" (Lowder). It was believed that if someone were genuinely sorry for their wrongdoings and confessed them to God, then God would forgive them.

The highest goal of both religions is to get rid of sin. Once they have gotten rid of sin, they will enter Nirvana for Buddhists and Heaven for Christians. The idea behind getting rid of evil is that you are in a state of pure happiness and God's grace (Lowder). However, these rewards are not instantaneous. You cannot just become a better person overnight and expect to gain entrance into Nirvana or Heaven. You must continue to try harder to reach your goals.

The idea behind peace as defined by Christianity is very different from the concept behind peace as defined by Buddhism. Christians believe that peace can only happen once God has been achieved (Roberts). Once you have found God, you will never have to worry about being at war with anyone or anything. "The Prince of Peace" is a term often used in Christianity. Those looking for this type of peace should follow Christ and accept his salvation (Roberts). This type of peace ends up being an instantaneous reward. It doesn't take Effort on the person's part, but they must accept that they will not be receiving it until their death (Roberts).

On the other hand, Buddhism believes that those who achieve Nirvana or Heaven will end up gaining a state of peace without ever having to worry about finding it (Wallis). "The peace that the Buddha teaches is not an external peace which crushes resistance: it is an inner peace, which arises from the removal of all desires and cravings" (Wallis). Once you have gained this type of peace, you will have reached Nirvana. The downside to this type of vacation is that we must continue to try harder to achieve it. Therefore, it is a continuous cycle of working towards our goal.

Overall, there are many defining similarities between Buddhism and Christianity. Overall, it starts with understanding each religion's views as a definition for sin and merit/demerit points. Christianity believes that all humans are sinners, but certain sins go against the Ten Commandments. These sins lead to the excommunication of those who commit them, and a scapegoat is used to explain why these sins occurred in the first place (Lowder).

If an action is committed, it leads only to suffering. Therefore, Buddhism focuses on doing good deeds to reach Nirvana (Wallis). They believe that once a person has attained Nirvana, they will have achieved peace and will no longer have to worry about being at war with anyone or anything (Wallis).

The Wheel of Dharma also plays a significant role in Buddhism and Christianity. The wheel represents different stages on the path of achieving Nirvana or Heaven (Wallis; Roberts). Both religions must continue to try harder to reach their goals (Wallis; Roberts) eventually. However, if a person believes in Christianity, they think they must do their part on the path to get to God, and it is their sin that prevents them from obtaining him (Lowder). If a person follows Buddhism, they believe that their merit and demerit points determine whether or not they are going the right way towards reaching Nirvana (Lowder).

Differences of Buddhism and Christianity

Buddhism and Christianity have many similarities and differences. Buddhism was developed in India to find enlightenment through self-discipline, which focuses on the self. Buddhist practice is less ritualized than Christian tradition but more individualistic. Buddhist monks live a life of voluntary poverty and are therefore dependent on their lay followers for contributions.

Christianity is rooted in Egypt, focusing on being saved from sin through Jesus Christ's sacrifice to appease God's wrath against humanity. A key difference is that Christianity focuses more heavily on ritual practices such as baptism and communion as part of the faith. In contrast, Buddhism focuses on spiritual practices such as meditation or mindfulness. Buddhism, like Christianity, does not advocate isolation from society but encourages positive action.

They follow his teachings and strive to go to heaven when they die. All life was characterized by grief, and all humans were trapped in what could be called a cycle of suffering. This cycle consists of birth, sickness, old age, and death. The path to be freed from suffering was Noble Eightfold Path: right views, right intention, right speech, right action, right livelihood, right Effort, right mindfulness, and right concentration. The historical Buddha did not have a teaching about the afterlife, and there is much disagreement among his followers about what happens after death.

The main difference between both religions comes with what happens after you do achieve your peace. There are many different religions, but the primary way to achieve peace is through Jesus (Roberts). Buddhists do not have a particular direction to follow to find peace. Instead, they believe that there are many ways of getting there.

It leads them to the idea of a continuous cycle. In addition to this, other differences between Christianity and Buddhism are the techniques used to obtain Nirvana or Heaven. In Christianity, you have Jesus, who provides an immediate reward once you accept his salvation. In Buddhism, there are many ways to achieve this type of peace. However, none of them can be performed until a person has tried hard enough.

Chapter 13:
How to Find Enlightenment

When a human being has satisfied his basic needs – food, water, shelter, security, and so on – he begins to wonder about the purpose of existence or the essence of life. The Buddha himself had reflected on this, especially as he may have been a noble whose basic needs were fully satisfied.

Helping Others

Buddhism teaches compassion because it enables one to value life in general. The Buddha himself chose to help guide others towards the path of Enlightenment because of mercy. To find the essence in life in this aspect, you may begin taking on a sense of responsibility for other beings, especially those who are in a more difficult position than you are. Perhaps you can volunteer for a local charity organization or use your skills for the welfare of others.

Cultivating the Four Divine Abodes

Meditation is the recommended way to cultivate the Four Divine Abodes, namely:

- Loving-kindness

- Compassion

- Sympathetic bliss, and

- Equanimity

In a quiet and peaceful place, spend some time reflecting on any of the Four Divine Abodes. For instance, if you will meditate on Loving-kindness, reflect on how to describe this feeling. Try to embrace this as part of who you are, and by meditating on them, you will find that your meditation has real purpose and that you come closer to understanding what enlightenment is.

Visualize a person in your life who can easily make you genuinely feel this quality. If you meditate on loving-kindness, you might think of a loved one you care for with all your heart. Often, these are the people who bring out the best in us. Through their actions and belief in you, you can see what it's like to incorporate these qualities into your life.

As you invoke the feeling of the quality, let it reverberate from within you to your surroundings. In the case of loving-kindness, you can visualize your loved ones and other people you do not usually care for in real life. Through practice, you could even direct it towards those whom you do not particularly like. The point of this is that you overcome your prejudices and make yourself capable of shutting off prejudice and seeing beyond it.

Continue to extend the feeling of the quality towards all beings in the world. Visualize it pouring from your heart towards them. You can continuously practice this form of meditation so that the Four Divine Abodes will eventually become more natural to you.

Embracing these qualities will then enable you to see the true essence of life. It helps you to become more optimistic. It allows you to increase your mindfulness and energy levels so that the energy you give off is positive and helps those around you see joy and happiness in their own lives.

Generosity

To be excellent means to be open to helping others without expecting anything in return. There are several ways to become more generous to others, but in traditional Buddhist teachings, there are four ways:

To share the teachings of the Buddha: Leading others towards a path that frees them from suffering is a great thing to do. It enables others to think and act for themselves and gain the right motivation to live a meaningful life. When you experience the positivity of your belief in Buddhism's philosophy, you can impart that to others and share with them the joy that this brings to your life. Each person must choose their route through life. You cannot select it for them. However, you can influence those you care about to learn the generosity of spirit from knowing you. Give without expectation of thanks or return. When you do, you feel nearer to the spiritual awakening than when you add strings to the things you give.

To protect other beings: Other living beings, humans and animals alike, have to live through life-threatening conditions every day. The only way for them to be saved is by helping those in better positions than they are. In day-to-day life, this could mean giving to the poor or being generous with your time when people are sick and in need of company. Extend your protection to people around you who are less well off than you.

To inspire and motivate others: You can also practice what you teach through meditation and follow the teachings of the Buddha. When others see that you are capable of it, they might be inspired to do the same. Inspiration does not involve any expectations. You can share what you know about Buddhism's teachings, but you cannot influence people to follow the way simply because you say so. They need to see your example and to be inspired by it, rather than being expected to follow a way that does not seem natural to them.

Offering material goods: Living beings need food, shelter, clothing, and other materials to improve their quality of life. Your generosity in the form of such gifts can tremendously benefit them. This way is easily most associated with the concept of altruism. In the Protestant and Catholic religions, people give alms. These are collections of money that are used for the benefit of the church or of other people. When you have things that you no longer need, there are always those who have less than you. Offering them the things you know will make their lives more comfortable should become a natural way forward for those who believe in Buddhist philosophy.

Moral Behavior

Moral behavior in exercising self-discipline so that you do not cause harm to other beings. The Effort placed into choosing the more difficult but morally upright path instead of the easy but wrong one is one way to uphold this Perfection. Another is to cultivate genuine compassion for others through prayer, meditation, and good work. Through constant practice, moral behavior will become more natural and spontaneous to you.

Patience

The more you practice the teachings of the Buddha, the more naturally patient you will be. Being patient protects yourself and others because it restrains you from allowing feelings such as ill will and anger to transform into destructive actions. As your patience continues to grow, you will notice that such negative emotions become weaker until you can no longer feel them.

To help you develop patience, here are traditional Buddhist practices to try:

Acknowledge and Accept Suffering: however, by accepting this reality, you develop the patience to go through these negative experiences. Through this, you do not become overwhelmed by feelings of regret, resentment, or anger associated with these events in your life. The acceptance of the Four Noble Truths will help you with this. The very first Noble Truth tells you that suffering is something that happens in life. However, when you strengthen your ability to accept suffering, you are more potent when such an event causes suffering.

Stay calm: staying calm despite frustrating or dangerous events leads to good karmic results. At first, it might be a challenge to remain calm when someone is attacking you. However, by taking a step back, you can analyze the best steps you can take based on the situation before you react.

Develop patience in pursuit: as you continue to practice the Buddha's teachings, there will be times when your old habits resurface and tempt you to steer from the path. However, you must remain patient in your efforts even if you do not always see immediate results. To do that, simply draw yourself back by reminding yourself of the teachings that have led you to start your journey in the first place.

Effort

Effort refers to one's commitment and perseverance in choosing to do what is right. It also means doing things with enthusiasm instead of feeling as if you are abstaining and resisting something. Some Buddhist teachers even emphasize that Effort is the foundation of the other Perfections because, with it, the rest would naturally fall into place.

To practice Effort, you must understand and acknowledge the presence of the three obstacles that impede it. These are defeatism, trivial pursuits, and laziness.

Chapter 14:
Combating Stress, Anxiety, and Depression with Buddhism

Suffering is an inevitable part of life and, until you have reached the state of Enlightenment, it helps to know how to cope with each challenge you face. Stressful situations can stir feelings of pain and anxiety, more so if they have to do with the things that you are most attached to. The good news is that Buddhist teachings can show you ways to cope with such emotions and events. The most effective of these is Mindfulness Meditation.

Mindfulness is the trait of paying close attention to the present moment. It allows you to see the reality for what it is, unclouded by assumptions and expectations. Studies show how effective mindfulness meditation is in reducing stress both instantaneously and over the long term. It triggers you to either face the problem or flees from it. In both cases, the body and mind react in the same way.

Consider the Best Ways to Respond to Stress and Anxiety

The body responds to how the mind perceives a stressful situation, so the best way to feel less stress is by calming the mind first. Therefore, the stronger your reason is, the more resistant your body would be towards stressful situations. Begin by recognizing your power to choose. For instance, you can use your journal to reflect on how you usually responded to these situations. There are plenty of healthy options. Here are some that are in line with the principles of Buddhism:

- Practice breathing meditation to regularize heart rate and breathing. You will find that this is covered in detail within the pages of this book.

- Go on walking mindfulness meditation to temporarily step away from the stressful situation and allow your mind to think deeply.

- Stay away from intoxicating substances that will only impede your judgment (particularly alcohol).

- Exercise with mindfulness to train the body to be more resistant.

- Detach yourself from the situation as if you are a mere spectator.

- Chant a mantra that helps strengthen your mind, such as "everything is going to be alright," or "I am calm and collected."

Once you have positive responses to stress and anxiety, you can then practice them regularly through meditation.

Breathing Meditation

Mindful breathing in and of itself merely is aware of your breath without changing it. Practicing it is a great way to acknowledge and express gratitude for the ability to breathe and help you regulate it during stressful situations.

Breathing meditation, on the other hand, can be done using a variety of techniques. One is deep breathing meditation, which is incredibly effective at reducing stress and anxiety. Here are the steps to do it:

1. Sit or lie down comfortably. Keep your back straight and shoulders relaxed. You can choose whether to use a hard chair and keep your feet planted flat on the floor or whether you want to use a cushion, bend your knees and cross your ankles. Your hands need to be posed, one cupped by the other with the palms facing upward and your thumbs touching each other.

2. Focus on your natural breath, noticing each movement of the body as the air passes through from your nostrils to the upper abdomen.

3. It will help you feel the air entering your body and create a pivot motion that will tell you that you live sufficiently profoundly.

4. Begin breathing deeply. As you inhale, notice how your belly rises, but not your chest. As you exhale, see how your stomach falls while the trunk remains relatively still. As you breathe, this movement should form a rhythm.

5. Another breathing meditation to try for stress and anxiety

relief is by counting your breaths. It helps you to relax and calm the mind as well as the body. Here are the steps. After a while of meditating in this manner, you may not need to count but will know the length of your breaths instinctively by the rhythm they form in the movement of your stomach.

Mindfulness in Walking Meditation

I have included this aspect of meditation because it is useful when away from home and facing stressful situations. You may find yourself having to meet with people who cause you stress or face a meeting that worries you. Walking meditation will help you overcome the fear and strengthen your mind to be clear-headed and meet whatever anxiety is calm.

1. Loosen any clothing that may be restrictive.
2. Stand with your back straight and start to take steps, with your head slightly lowered, watching each movement of your feet.
3. Breathe in, move the foot forward, and be aware of all the foot muscles' movement.
4. Feel your other foot lift off the ground, move forward, be conscious of the muscles' movement in the leg, the knee, and the calf.
5. Be conscious of the foot touching the ground and continue to breathe in and out using your nostrils for the inhalation and

feeling the air go through to your lower chest area.

6. When you breathe out, move your leg in time with the breath so that you are always in rhythm with your breathing.

7. Think of nothing else at all. If thoughts happen, let them slide away into the background and go back to your concentration on walking and meditating.

This kind of meditation helps you alleviate the types of stressors brought about by events in life. Interviews, meeting new people, or going to a meeting can all be precursors to this kind of stress, and this type of meditation can help you keep your composure and control what you are feeling inside of yourself. Be in the moment. Be in the steps that you take. Breathe.

Be Mindful of Your Thought Patterns

Modern-day stressors are not the leading cause of your stress and anxiety. It has more to do with your perspectives. The teachings of the Buddha offer plenty of ways to transform your thought patterns for the better. However, anyone can get distracted from these because of the demands of daily life. See things from a different angle.

Imagine yourself in someone else's shoes, such as someone you admire (perhaps the Buddha himself?). How do you think this person would perceive the situation? How would he respond to the source of stress? Sometimes this exercise can change how you see things yourself. You may have already done this in your everyday

day-to-day life. I am thinking as a child thinking that I was a concert pianist when I had piano practice, and it's almost the same thing, except that you are using that other person as your focal point and looking at the situation from the angle that person would see it, rather than seeing it as yourself. It helps you to avoid distraction and to use inspiration to guide you.

Identify the Individual Parts of the Stressor.

Seeing a big issue as a whole can be taxing, emotionally and mentally. Therefore, it would be a good idea to break the subject down into smaller, more manageable parts so that you can stop procrastinating and start solving it. It may hurt you to think about the things that stress you initially, but when you can identify them and dissect the problem into smaller portions, it is easier to cope with. We put off dealing with stressors because, in themselves, they cause us stress, and we believe in avoidance.

However, if you dissect the problems, they become smaller and more manageable, and you can gradually expose yourself to these stressors so that they don't cause the same psychological damage. Let me give you an instance. If you have problems with relationships, write down the issues in a list format and work on one of them at a time until they become less of a problem. If you are stressed by going into a public place, try entering an area where you are more aware of who is likely to be there and gradually spread your wings a little and include new people into your circle so that you are not so anxious with strangers.

Consult an Expert

If you acknowledge that you alone are incapable of solving your stress and anxiety problem, do not be afraid to approach an expert. Receiving guidance from someone who has already gained the wisdom to solve such problems will benefit you greatly and enable you to solve the problem for yourself later on in life. The subconscious mind works when you have stressors because it responds to how your mind has taught it to respond. You can change this programming by mild exposure to the trigger and gradually realize that you can react positively to whatever that trigger is. Professionals help people to do this if they are afraid of doing it on their own.

Christianity Over the Years

Christianity refers to many religious traditions that have grown from a single source. These include Catholicism, Protestantism (which has many divisions), Copts, Eastern Orthodox Christianity, and countless small sects. All of them have in common the teachings of Jesus Christ as they have evolved over the past 2,000 years. Christianity has had an incalculable effect on the world, both on its culture and language and its political and social development. Western governments have established national holidays around Christian rituals, and we live by a calendar that measures time according to "Before Christ" and "Anno Domini" (in the year of Our Lord).

Chapter 15:
Mudras to Combat Stress

We live in an age of anxiety. When we are stressed, we acknowledge it yet still refuse to address our stressors like they're the plague. This fallacy leads us on a continual cycle: experiencing more stress and more tension, leading to fatigue, physical illness, or worse. It's time for you to take charge!

What Does Mundras Mean?

Mudras are a type of symbolic hand gesture in Hinduism and Buddhism. While there are many different mudras, each one represents something about the religion. In Hinduism, people often use mudras to show spiritual powers or blessings and represent aspects of the god or goddess they worship. Buddhists may use a mudra to represent Buddha's teaching and serve as an offering during meditation. In yoga, mudras are used to help balance the body.

Mudra means "seal" or "sign." A mudra can be made with any part of the body, but most commonly, it is made with the hands or fingers. Often a mudra is incorporated into a yantra, which symbolizes a sacred diagram and has a specific set of hand postures. Yantras represent cosmic principles that create and sustain the world; they are used for meditative purposes by Hindus and Buddhists.

It is said that through the use of mudras and yantras, the body can be purified and aligned with the universe. By using mudras, people are believed to increase their energy and creativity.

By incorporating specific mudras into your daily routine (they can be practiced anywhere!), you will learn how to manage your stressful lifestyle while simultaneously improving your physical and mental well-being.

If you're feeling stressed, have a hard time sleeping, or need some help increasing your self-confidence, try these mudras! Mudras are hand gestures that can help with physical and emotional ailments. They can also provide more peace of mind if you're worried about an upcoming event.

Different Mudras to Help Physical and Emotional Stress

1. Gyan mudra: Place your right thumb and middle finger on your forehead and press the tip of your ring finger against the advice of your thumb to form a circle. Hold it for as long as possible for the best effect.

2. Ashwini mudra: Alternately press your ring finger and thumb tips against each other while you keep the rest of your fingers extended. Inhale deeply and hold for five to ten seconds.

3. Gyan mudra with Anahata chakra mudra: Place your right hand in the Gyan mudra, but instead of touching your forehead, connect the middle of your chest with it. Make an Anahata chakra mudra with the rest of your fingers (see below), and hold it for as long as

possible.

4. Bhand Mudra: The Bhand Mudra is similar to holding a ball under your hand or cupping it from underneath.

5. Anahata chakra mudra: Interlock all of your fingers except for your index and pinky fingers. Straighten them out while you keep them touching. The pinky finger should extend straight out, while the rest should be bent at a 90-degree angle.

6. Gyan mudra with Sushumna Anahata Chakra mudra: Use both hands to make each mudra as described above, then hold them together (as if in prayer) against your chest with the fingertips touching or overlapping slightly.

7. Bharam: Place your hands, palms facing upwards, and fingers slightly separated on the sides of your face.

8. Antakshari mudra: Point your middle finger at someone else, then wiggle it at them while you make that hand gesture with your other hand right after. Do it repeatedly quickly for best effect!

9. Gyan mudra with closed eyes: As in Gyan mudra, this time with closed eyes and one hand closed around the other fist when tonguing through the lips.

10. Gyan mudra with Anahata chakra mudra: As in the description above, use a Gyan mudra instead of touching your chest.

11. Gyan mudra with Sushumna Anahata Chakra mudra: As in the description above, but use both hands to make each mudra as described above, then hold them together (as if in prayer) against

your chest with the fingertips touching or overlapping slightly.

12. Bharam: Place your hand's palms down on either side of your head and press hard enough so that you feel some pressure while keeping the two palms facing each other and fingers apart.

13. Gyan mudra with closed eyes: As in Gyan mudra, this time with closed eyes and one hand closed around the other fist when tonguing through the lips.

14. Gyan mudra with Sushumna Anahata Chakra mudra: As in the description above, but use both hands to make each mudra as described above, then hold them together (as if in prayer) against your chest with the fingertips touching or overlapping slightly.

15. Gyan mudra with Anahata chakra mudra: As in the description above, use a Gyan mudra instead of touching your chest.

16. Bharam: Place your hand's palms down on either side of your head and press hard enough so that you feel some pressure while keeping the two palms facing each other and fingers apart.

17. Gyan mudra with closed eyes: As in Gyan mudra, this time with closed eyes and one hand closed around the other fist when tonguing through the lips.

18. Gyan mudra with Sushumna Anahata Chakra mudra: As in the description above, but use both hands to make each mudra as described above, then hold them together (as if in prayer) against your chest with the fingertips touching or overlapping slightly.

19. Gyan mudra with Anahata chakra mudra: As in the description

above, use a Gyan mudra instead of touching your chest.

20. Bharam: Place your hand's palms down on either side of your head and press hard enough so that you feel some pressure while keeping the two palms facing each other and fingers apart.

21. Antakshari mudra: Point your middle finger at someone else, then wiggle it at them while you make that hand gesture with your other hand right after. Do it repeatedly quickly for best effect!

22. Gyan mudra with closed eyes: As in Gyan mudra, this time with closed eyes and one hand closed around the other fist when tonguing through the lips.

23. Gyan mudra with Sushumna Anahata Chakra mudra: As in the description above, but use both hands to make each mudra as described above, then hold them together (as if in prayer) against your chest with the fingertips touching or overlapping slightly.

24. Bharam: Place your hand's palms down on either side of your head and press hard enough so that you feel some pressure while keeping the two palms facing each other and fingers apart.

25. Gyan mudra with Anahata chakra mudra: As in the description above, use a Gyan mudra instead of touching your chest.

26. Gyan mudra with closed eyes: As in Gyan mudra, this time with closed eyes and one hand closed around the other fist when tonguing through the lips.

27. Gyan mudra with Sushumna Anahata Chakra mudra: As in the description above, but use both hands to make each mudra as

described above, then hold them together (as if in prayer) against your chest with the fingertips touching or overlapping slightly.

28. Bharam: Place your hand's palms down on either side of your head and press hard enough so that you feel some pressure while keeping the two palms facing each other and fingers apart.

29. Gyan mudra with Anahata chakra mudra: As in the description above, use a Gyan mudra instead of touching your chest.

30. Bharam: Place your hand's palms down on either side of your head and press hard enough so that you feel some pressure while keeping the two palms facing each other and fingers apart.

31. Gyan mudra with Anahata chakra mudra: As in the description above, use a Gyan mudra instead of touching your chest.

32. Bharam: Place your hand's palms down on either side of your head and press hard enough so that you feel some pressure while keeping the two palms facing each other and fingers apart.

33. Gyan mudra with Anahata chakra mudra: As in the description above, use a Gyan mudra instead to touch your chest.

34. Bharam: Place your hand's palms down on either side of your head and press hard enough so that you feel some pressure while keeping the two palms facing each other and fingers apart.

35. Gyan mudra with Anahata chakra mudra: As in the description above, use a Gyan mudra instead of touching your chest.

36. Bharam: Place your hand's palms down on either side of your

head and press hard enough so that you feel some pressure while keeping the two palms facing each other and fingers apart.

37. Gyan mudra with Anahata chakra mudra: As in the description above, use a Gyan mudra instead of touching your chest.

38-53 Repeat steps 13-37 three more times, always starting with 13 and 53.

54. Shambhavi mudra: This is the same as Gyan Mudra, except that you use your right hand to form the Gyan mudra and your left hand to form shambhavi mudra.

55-57 Repeat steps 13-37 three more times, always starting with 13 and ending with 57.

58. Utkanthi mudra: Keep both hands open and upturned.

Repeat steps 13-37 three more times, always starting with 13 and ending with 61. The "C" is the center. Each of the 13 numbers is assigned a letter. The numbers from 1 to 9 are designated A, B, C, D, E, F; the numbers 10 to 90 are assigned G, H, I, J, K; and the numbers 100 to 999 are assigned L. For example, 4225 is 5 (J) and 23 (L).

Purpose of the Mudras

The purpose of a mudra in Hinduism is to prevent evil influences from entering the body through the hands and encourage good energy from holy figures to enter the body. The hands are believed to link to one's heart directly, so they are seen as an avenue for sending love and receiving love. As part of prayers or rituals, mudras have been used since ancient times in Hinduism.

Different types of mudra involve different finger positions. Some might use a single fist position, while others may include the thumb or entire fist to create an almost meditative state. The mudra is supposed to bring about divine energy, healing, and blessing, all with one simple gesture of the hands.

A mudra can be performed with a hands-on lap while sitting. A mudra can also be performed during a conversation or even when holding a pen or pencil.

Ancient yogis studied how the mind responds when one uses mudras and recited mantras using specific hand gestures, such as "Gyan Mudra" (the motion used when chanting the mantra "Om Gum Ganapataye Namaha," meaning Glory Be to Lord Ganesh).

Mudras are still commonly used in Hinduism to bring about positive life changes and to deliver a message that a person wants to communicate to the world.

Chapter 16:
Start Your Day with Positive Motivations and Thoughts

It is imperative to incorporate values and principles into our daily lives. It ensures peace and tranquility in the world. Living each day mindfully will not be comfortable in the beginning. You may feel the need to give up. However, living mindfully is the only way to solve issues we face in our daily lives.

Man must learn to be at peace because everything in this world keeps changing with time. He must understand that expecting something to last forever will only bring forth distress.

Pursuit of Happiness

Life is often seen as the pursuit of happiness. The yearning for pleasure is an instinct. Nobody wants to be unhappy. When a person is happy, he wants the feeling to last forever. He does everything within his capacity to maintain it. When a person is unhappy, he tries to push the feeling away.

He either broods about it or thinks of ways to forget the factor that's making him sick. Every other desire of a human being is incidental and ancillary to the desire for happiness. Man seeks money, wealth, company, and other aspects to attain happiness. However, Buddha said, "there is no path to happiness. Happiness is the path itself".

Letting Go of Clinging

When we are happy or have something we like, we tend to make it last forever. We do not want to accept that the world is dynamic. We do not want to get change. Similarly, when we are facing something negative, we are scared that it will last forever. A real Buddhist would know otherwise.

Don't Take it Personally

"Why did this happen to me?" We ask ourselves and the people around us when things do not go our way. We are demanding explanations for why something negative has happened to us. The only practical answer is that negativity and misfortune may be bestowed on anybody. There is no need to take this personally. Instead, realize that the suffering is only temporary and move on in life.

Opening up to Love

Buddha, in his sermons, emphasized the importance of love. He said that the best and most important kind of love is one's love for oneself. Only when one loves oneself will one be able to love another. It is genuine. It is not possible to share something you do not possess. If a man does not love himself, then there is no love inside him. He will not be able to love others. We are often distressed and upset about "not being loved."

Sometimes people are sad because the person from whom they crave love does not love them back enough. It causes suffering. The sting of love can be the worst and most unbearable pain in the world. It is why people are often scared to open up to love or to expect love. If love can hurt us so much, why does Buddha ask us to be open to love? Perhaps the reason is that Buddha's definition of love is different from ours, or maybe because he understands this emotion's depth far more than we do.

When you love someone and expect them to love you back the same way, such love can no longer be called selfless. If love isn't selfless, it isn't loved at all. It is merely attachment. It is the attachment that causes pain and not loves. The Bible says that love is patient, kind, selfless, and all-forgiving. Being able to love that way is putting an end to a lot of suffering that we endure.

Buddha advocated the Love Kindness meditation to help people develop this ability. This meditation focuses on nourishing the feelings of love and compassion in your heart. The Buddha asked his disciples to meditate on someone they love. However, he asked them to ensure that their focus must be on the emotion of love and not on the person they are thinking of. Men must strive to foster the feeling of compassion within them. They must feel for other fellow beings. Man must realize that the whole world is his family and that every other deserves to be loved.

Buddha said that hate is not an answer to anything. Hatred, greed, and ignorance are the main reasons for suffering in this world. Man must develop the ability to love and take care of another as much as he loves himself. It will ensure peaceful co-existence between beings. It can change the reason for one's existence, to redefine every aspect of him once and for all. Only the rays of love can warm a cold soul or heal a broken heart.

Love has the power to open the inner eye and to fill one with bliss and peace. However, one must have the insight to differentiate between love and attachment. It was able to make this distinction that will change one's life forever.

Anger Management

One day a young boy fought with his mother. He said things that he didn't mean because of his anger. It left his mother deeply wounded. The young boy's father, who had listened to the mother and son's conversation, called the boy aside and walked him to the wooden fence guarding their home. He asked the boy not to speak when he is angry. The son did as he was told. After a few days, the boy ran out of pins. When the young boy confronted his father, the father asked the boy to remove the nails one by one from the fence whenever he was angry. Once again, the boy took his father's advice.

Freedom from Fear

We live in fear every day. Fear of death, fear of losing someone we love, fear of being poor, fear of being unsuccessful, etc. These are only some of the fears we face every day. Living in fear is as good as being half alive.

When we are in a good state, we are scared of losing it. When we are in a bad state, we fear it will last forever. The most profound reason for this is desire. It is our desire to be happy always and our desire never to be sad. However, this is an impossible goal to achieve. Further, there is no way to put an end to suffering. Old age and death are also unavoidable in life; there is absolutely no point in dreading them.

A Compassionate Life

Compassion is the highest level of love and kindness. Buddhism stresses the importance of developing love and service in one's life. Understanding also means "empathy to other beings." Man must feel sympathetic to other fellow beings. He must pay special attention to increase positive feelings like love and kindness within him.

Similarly, man must make a conscious effort to ensure that negative feelings are discarded from the mind. Man must have to ability to move beyond self-centeredness. It is easier to be compassionate when one realizes that his fellow beings also have wants and needs. They also want happiness and companionship.

Chapter 17:
How Do I Begin to Practice Buddhism?

The Five Precepts of Buddhism are the fundamental ethical guidelines for Buddhists. However, they are not regarded as a rigid set of rules and gentle suggestions on living a life free from suffering. After all, the Buddha always emphasizes the being's power of choice.

Below is a description of the Five Precepts as well as suggestions on how to put each of them into practice:

The First Precept: do not intentionally kill any living being

The followers of Buddha should not entertain the idea of causing harm or, worse, killing any other living beings, whether human or animal. Instead, they cultivate genuine concern for and loving-kindness towards the welfare of others.

You can bring the First Precept to mind each time you are tempted to hurt a living being, be it an insect or another person. The least you can do is avoid having anything to do with the senseless killing of animals, such as for sport or overconsumption. It is this First Precept that has inspired many Buddhists to become vegan.

The Second Precept: take only what is given to you

This precept greatly discourages stealing and "borrowing" items from others without returning them. By following this precept, Buddhists seek equality in the distribution of resources, and, at the same time, they wish to instill the value of generosity in themselves.

To put the Second Precept into practice in the modern world, you can work towards living within your means and paying off debts that you owe. Many Buddhists have turned to the minimalist lifestyle because it guides people to let go of consumerism and live meaningful lives. In this day and age, this is also a common practice because the simplicity of this precept is that it gives so much back. The common saying that "less is more" really comes into its own when examining how it applies to modern-day living.

The Third Precept: do not misuse the senses

In the traditional sense, the third precept advises against letting one's sexual drive dominate one's life, as it is understood that it leads to suffering. Instead, Buddhists are encouraged to live a contented life with thoughts and actions that serve a meaningful purpose.

However, you may interpret the Third Precept as something that encompasses all abuse of the senses. For instance, it can be taken as advice against overeating, which leads to many sufferings, such as obesity. Instead, the Buddhist is guided towards doing things (including food consumption) in moderation and useful purposes.

Misuse of the senses can include an excess of anything that causes suffering. Excess drug consumption, excess smoking, or any quantity that touches the senses is considered to be against this precept.

The Fourth Precept: do not speak of falsehood

The Buddha teaches that one should not lie, slander, and engage in malicious gossip. Instead, one should only speak words of truth and kindness and be motivated by positive intentions when engaging in a conversation with others.

It can be tempting at times to talk negatively about something. However, now that you have learned of this Precept, perhaps you can practice mindfulness in the way you speak. If you find it hard to hold yourself back from saying things that could hurt others, you might want to consider writing in a diary. It is a great way to begin acknowledging and monitoring your thoughts before turning them into spoken words.

It is hard for people to accept that hurtful thing you say to people comes back to you and hurts you as much as those to whom the words were directed. By being true to yourself and kind to others, you suffer less, and you can feel better about who you are. Your journal is simply a means to record your negativity so that you don't make the same mistake again.

The Fifth Precept: avoid intoxicants

The Fifth Precept emphasizes the harm caused by drinking alcohol and taking unnecessary stimulants and drugs. Buddhists are on the path towards improving their concentration and cultivating rational thought. Therefore, this precept is a gentle reminder of what causes the opposite of these. However, following them rests solely on your own volition, especially since the Buddha encourages everyone to think and experience things for themselves rather than to follow through blind faith.

The Five Precepts are reasonably straightforward and logical for people to follow and help put mindfulness in your life. Note them down in short form to be reminded of them and correct your behavior when you see yourself being taken away from them by life in general. Your awareness of these Precepts makes you more responsible for your actions. By accepting these seriously, you lessen your suffering and control how your mind can perceive mindfulness.

Chapter 18:
Review of the 5 Precepts of Buddhism?

In total, there are ten precepts; however, the first five are practiced by all Buddhists with the last five generally only practiced by those who are working toward a monastic life. These precepts are meant to help you achieve your highest status of awakening. These precepts are keys for Buddhists who are meditating so they can focus on their meditation with a clear mind and create a more simple daily routine. We have covered them previously but let's look a bit closer.

Do Not Kill

When it comes to animals, Buddhists believe that it is worse to kill larger animals than smaller ones because the bigger the animal is, the more effort it takes to kill it. This precept is to help you focus on compassion, stating that no matter what, you should not harm a living thing even if it harms you.

There are five factors involved, a living thing, the perception of the living thing, the thought of killing the living being, the action of killing the living being, and the result, which is death. There are also ways in which the action can be carried out. These ways include missiles, slow poisoning, psychic powers, sorcery, instigation, and one's own hands

Do Not Steal

Buddhists want to keep themselves from stealing someone else's possessions. They also want to avoid such things as economic exploitation and fraud. This precept not only means that people should not steal items from their neighbor's house or a store, but it also includes not taking rides from a city bus for free. Not paying for your ride is the same as taking a possession that doesn't belong to you. This process involves five factors: (1) something belonging to someone else, (2) knowing the item belongs to someone else, (3) thinking of stealing the item, (4) the performance of the action, and (5) stealing as a result of the action.

Do Not Lie

Many people refer to the precept of "Do not lie" as "Don't gossip," "Don't call people names," and "Don't say anything false against anyone else." These offenses range from small to severe. A small offense would be a Buddhist telling someone that he doesn't have the item someone asked him for when the Buddhist has that item. A larger or more severe offense is to say you saw something when you didn't see the action, such as stating you saw your neighbor take someone's lawn ornament when in fact you have not seen him or her take it. Like with the other precepts, there are four steps involved when it comes to lying. The first step is something which isn't so. The second step is thinking about deception. The third step is taking the effort to carry it out. The fourth step is actually stating this lie to someone else.

Do Not Misuse Sex

Misusing sex means different things to different groups of people. For instance, for monks and nuns, it means that they shouldn't engage in sexual acts. For people who are married, it means that they shouldn't commit adultery. Committing unlawful acts are also a part of misusing sex.

There are at least ten other groups of people, usually women, who shouldn't be a part of sexual activities due to unlawful nature. One of these groups consists of women who are bought with money, like prostitutes. Other groups include temporary wives, kept women, and women in war. Buddhists also believe that concubine women fall into the "misuse of sex" category if these women are being used for the fun of having sex, such as an extramarital affair.

Do Not Consume Alcohol or Other Drugs

The biggest reason why Buddhists believe you need to stay away from drugs and alcohol is that these are known to cloud the mind. In order to reach your full enlightenment, you need to have a clear mind. If your mind is clouded or you can't think clearly, you won't be able to obtain the clear mind you need to move down your path. While they don't consider prescription drugs to be part of this precept, they do consider social drinking to be a part of it.

Some Buddhists have even started to insist that other addictions can be considered drugs that cloud our minds—for example, addiction to our devices, such as computers, television, and smartphones. They state that these devices cloud our minds because they take us away from the reality of the world.

While many people don't feel that this precept will be helpful at first, after they have followed it for a while, they state that it helps them attain an amazing experience. People feel that their minds really do become clearer the more they keep away from drinking and any sort of drugs. They further state that they no longer find it strange or awkward to be one of the few people at social events who don't drink. People quickly come to realize that they won't be judged in any way if they keep from drinking even at a social level.

By not consuming drugs or alcohol, you don't corrupt your mind. Buddhists think of their minds as a sponge. Everything that you put into it, such as TV shows or video games, will corrupt your mind. Over time, this will begin to make you miserable because you have lost sight of what's really important as your mind has become cloudy.

Five Additional Activities for Certain Groups

Some people, such as those who are in the middle of preparing for monastic life or not within a family, need to add five more activities that they need to keep away from, along with the five precepts listed above. For Buddhists who are preparing for their lifestyle as monks and nuns, this is simply a means to help them attain the self-discipline they need within their monastic life.

For Buddhists who are preparing for the monk and nun lifestyle, they can eat between dawn and noon, usually only a small meal or two. The reason behind this is that they need to learn self-discipline, and not eating during certain times allows them to focus more on meditation. Another reason for this is to help them avoid excessive eating, which usually occurs in the evening during supper.

While Buddhists prepare for the monastic life, they are not to engage in forms of entertainment, such as singing, dancing, watching TV, and music. These behaviors can lead to clouding the mind, which is something that all Buddhists are supposed to stay away from. By keeping away from anything that clouds the mind, Buddhists are more likely to be able to focus on their meditation and work on their self-discipline. Taking part in these types of entertainments can also give Buddhists certain senses that will make it hard for them to keep away from sexual pleasures.

For this precept, you don't want to wear perfume, garlands, or any other type of personal adornment, such as makeup. Like when Buddhists keep away from such things as entertainment, they are keeping away from the use of perfumes and the like to help train the mind. The purpose of reaching your ultimate goal in your path of enlightenment is to keep a clear mind so you can focus on meditation and finding your inner peace. Another reason those aiming to enhance their self-discipline or preparing for the life of a nun or monk stay away from these items is that they can arouse senses that can lead to sexual pleasure.

This precept means that monks and nuns are to keep themselves at a level that is respectful for those who are above them. If they are to take high seats, it could boost their ego, and this won't help them in their path to enlightenment. They should not come to believe they are at a higher status.

Accepting Gold or Silver

This final precept ties into the previous one. Some Buddhists need to keep away from items that are gold and silver because these items are meant for people of higher status. By accepting gold and silver, they are letting in bad feelings within their body that can cause them to lose focus on their meditation and steer off their path of enlightenment.

It's important to remember that these precepts don't focus on whether you like something or not. They are put in place and practiced to help you stay on your path of enlightenment. They help you reach your true liberation, just as Buddha did. These precepts are placed because they have been known to help other Buddhists.

They can help you keep a clear mind so that you can focus on meditation, which is a piece of this puzzle that will help you remain calm and find not only happiness but also wisdom. They aren't meant to directly test your limits on what you believe you can or can't do. They are here to help guide you. Everyone stumbles every now and then, and no one says that if you stumble on these precepts, specifically the first five, that you won't be able to continue on your path of enlightenment. These are here to help you build your self-discipline while on your path.

Chapter 19:
Why is Buddhism so Popular?

Well, one reason is because of its similarity with Christianity. It's becoming more popular because of the connections it has with other religions in this country, such as Hinduism and Jainism. With more people following the faith, there might be more spread of misinformation about Buddhism's history.

Buddhism is increasingly the world's most popular religion. With some 6.2 billion people, it accounts for about half of the world's population. At one time, Buddhism was mainly a product of India; now, it's practiced in more than 110 countries worldwide and accounted for as many as two-fifths of all active followers of non-Christian faiths. It is estimated that there are between 235 million to 600 million Buddhists in China alone, but the country does not officially recognize any religion other than Christianity, Islam, and Taoism. (Wikipedia)

The rapid growth of the number of Buddhists in the world is obvious. Unlike many different religions, Buddhism presents no supernatural claims; it has no theology and does not ask its followers to accept anything on faith. It is entirely based on observation and reason. It makes Buddhism very easy to understand and follow.

Buddhism is a rational religion that appeals to people who are accustomed to a scientific way of thinking. The Buddha explained his findings in simple terms without using any supernatural concepts.

Buddhism emphasizes following the middle path. It discourages overindulgence in sensual pleasures as well as excess in self-denial. The Buddha showed a practical and balanced way of achieving real happiness.

The Four Noble Truths and The Eight-Fold Path summarize Buddhism's essence most practically so that one can practice and achieve inner peace even in this very life.

The Buddha's message applies to all people, irrespective of their birth, gender, color or caste, etc. He has not given any special privilege to any particular group of people.

The eightfold path is a universal guide that applies to people of all races and nations. It shows a practical way leading to the ultimate happiness.

Buddhism offers excellent hope because it teaches that everyone can achieve enlightenment in this very life. After death, one merges back into the infinite consciousness and achieves Nirvana. Hence the real essence of "self" never dies, and there is no fear of death or any other worries regarding it. It asks them to observe and verify its claims on their own and come to a rational conclusion based upon this observation. Thus, it appeals to people who like to think for themselves without blindly following any authority figure or dogma.

When you enter a Buddhist temple, you'll see numerous statues, incense being burned, flowers being offered, and monks prostrating themselves in front of the altar. Buddhists do not worship Buddhas in the same way as followers of other faiths worship their gods. Prostration in Buddhism is performed as a conscientious deed as opposed to being a mindless ritualistic act.

As we know these things in a few other significant religions, worshiping and idolization would be somewhat contradictory to Buddhism's core principles. Whereas Islam, Christianity, and the like worship Gods that are perceived as eternal, omnipresent, omnipotent, and unchanging, Buddhism perceives everything in this universe, except Nirvana, to be impermanent and essentially meaningless, as you will learn in detail later on. Therefore, it could be more accurate to consider Buddhism as a form of utmost dedication and devotion to the truth instead of an idol or divine ruler and creator.

More so than worship, the Buddha himself is simply respected and admired for his achievements. You can think of Buddhism as a large club of devout followers dedicated to carrying on the torch and preserving what they believe in, and It has been the most enlightened way of comprehending the world and life itself. The Buddha set an example that is followed voluntarily, but much more important than the man himself is each journey that those who seek awakening will travel.

The whole of Buddhist commitment is a very earthly attitude toward a worldly achievement attributed to a born man and has died like everyone else. What sets the Buddha apart is how he lived that entirely natural life and passed on knowledge to those who cared to listen, and that is what Buddhism is all about.

Conclusion

Buddhism is about the teachings of the Buddha. Buddhist centers are for beginners and established Buddhists alike. The atmosphere is welcoming because that is the way of the Buddhist – love, kindness, and compassion. There will be plenty of written information you can take home with you to study on your own. There will be Buddhist teachers to assist you in understanding all the teachings. You will learn how to meditate, an essential aspect of Buddhism. The reason that it is always best to seek out a practiced Buddhist for teachings is because there is only so much information and understanding you can take from books and articles. Having a teacher to discuss your studies can be a great tool for traveling down the path to enlightenment with more ease.

As you begin your path to enlightenment, you need to learn you can about Buddhism. There are different paths to enlightenment, so you must study each one to find the path that fits your life. The different paths of Buddhism usually have the same basic ideas but incorporate their own understandings of the Buddha's teachings. So, you will find variances between the paths. There are thousands of books available to teach you about Buddhism. It is important to focus on one aspect at a time. If you try to cram in all the Buddha's teachings as fast as you can, you are never going to understand what you are learning. You will also likely just get overwhelmed, leading you to give up on Buddhism.

A Buddhist teacher can help you with so many questions and aspects of Buddhism, so you make the best choice for you. A teacher can also monitor your readings and studying, so you stay focused. However, not everyone has immediate access to a Buddhist center, so you may need to make the first step on your own. Choose a specific aspect of Buddhism to study and learn. You want to absorb absolutely all of the knowledge until you have a complete understanding. Only then should you move on to another aspect. Take your time with your studies. Utilize the internet to find other Buddhists who will answer your questions and guide you on your path.

You can start off slow, simply learning some basic Buddhist terminology. You can start at the beginning and delve deep into the story of the Buddha and the origins of Buddhism. The goal is to choose a place to start, stick with it until you really understand it, and then move on to another area of study.

Some people want to immerse themselves in Buddhism from the beginning as they are just that excited to go down the path of enlightenment. However, others choose to take a more cautious journey, taking their time with the teachings, asking all the hard questions, and gaining as much insight as possible before taking even one more step. You decide how you want to learn about Buddhism as you are the only one who knows what is best for you.

Community is a crucial part of Buddhism. Buddhists need each other to learn from for guidance. You need a strong, smart support system during your path to Nirvana. You cannot learn all you need to learn alone. There are plenty of Buddhist forums, groups, websites, etc. full of practicing Buddhists who will provide you with the encouraging support system you need. They will also give you a place to ask your questions, quell your anxieties and concerns, and learn how to release them. Online groups can even help you with meditation.

One way you can bring Buddhism into your everyday life is to take the time to sit every day. Sitting in peace and quiet is a first step towards mindful meditation. If you cannot sit still for a few minutes each day, then you have to keep practicing. Meditation requires a stillness of the body and mind. So, start off with just sitting quietly. Ensure you can sit still for a bit of time. Start with five minutes each day. As you become more comfortable with just sitting in peace, add more time to each session. Eventually, you can start to bring meditation into the session.

Since Buddhism is a way of living your life, you have to be prepared to make many changes, especially in your awareness and understanding of the world around you and of your own mind. Awareness is a key point of Buddhism, so learning a proper meditation method is ideal. You must be able to clear your mind and attain a level of purity that will lead you to enlightenment.

You can practice meditation at home, on your own, with information you learn about meditation. You can practice meditation in a group setting with other blossoming Buddhists. You will likely find online groups where you can meditate "virtually" with a group. As long as you learn how to meditate, and you go further and further with each session in reaching that supreme level of a pure mind, then you are on the right track to enlightenment.

To bring Buddhism into your everyday life other than studying and meditation, just start living a kind and compassionate life. You want to put forth positive, happy energy in everything you do because, as you know, karma is watching. So, live your life knowing that karma will always find you. You are going to struggle during your Buddhism journey. There are going to be negative times as you learn more and more about the true nature of reality.

You will likely have to face some hard truths about yourself and the way that you live or feel. Just keep going forward. You are not going to become a full-fledged, enlightened Buddhist in just a few weeks or months. You are looking at years of studying and practicing and changing and living your new life before you reach Nirvana.

While this probably sounds overwhelming, it will be worth the effort and the wait. Once you reach the level of enlightenment, you will no longer struggle with letting go of clinging, with accepting that all things change, with living a simple life, and with total awareness. You will be awakened – you will be like the Buddha. You will have a full understanding of your mind, your life, and your actions, as well as your feelings and thoughts. You will be a Buddhist, and your future will be very bright.

www.ingramcontent.com/pod-product-compliance
Lightning Source LLC
Chambersburg PA
CBHW071518080526
44588CB00011B/1478